CON~~CILIUM~~

CONCILIUM 2019/1

The City and Global Development: Beyond the North-South Paradigm

Edited by

Edited by Linda Hogan, Alina Krause and
Markus Büker

Published in 2019 by SCM Press, 3rd Floor, Invicta House, 108–114 Golden Lane, London EC1Y 0TG.

SCM Press is an imprint of Hymns Ancient & Modern Ltd (a registered charity) 13A Hellesdon Park Road, Norwich NR6 5DR, UK

www.concilium.in

ISBN 978-0-334-03152-9

Printed in the UK by
Ashford, Hampshire

Concilium is published in March, June, August, October, December

Contents

Editorial

Global Development in an Increasingly Urbanised World

The 2030 Agenda and the Paris Agreement commit the international community to significant and extensive changes in order to address the current threats to life and coexistence, before it is too late. There is a certain consensus regarding the reasons why this is necessary. Humanity is crossing planetary boundaries. For example: The prevailing carbon- and resource-intensive systems of production and ways of life are unsustainable. Refugees from the Middle East and Africa mean that the global problems of wars, state failure and a lack of prospects are visible on the doorsteps of people in Europe. The emergence worldwide of authoritarian governments and populist movements, and in some cases right-wing extremism, calls the functionality of traditional democracies into question. How can we ensure that all human beings are able to live in an intact natural and social environment, and that no one is left behind? Everyone – each according to his or her specific responsibilities and means – is called upon to play a part in developing joint solutions that embrace all continents, religions and social strata. What role do religions play in this context?

For many decades the commitment to development aid and co-operation has been considered a case of distributive justice or charity on the part of a 'developed North' towards an 'underdeveloped South'. It was understood as 'catch-up development', meaning that the 'poor South' was to open up to an existing model, and to integrate into the prevailing system of the early industrialised countries in the so-called 'developed North', which is based on capitalism and market fundamentalism. Today, this understanding is no longer tenable. It is not just knowledge of the complex causal mechanisms linking 'development' and 'underdevelopment' that place the relationship between the North and the South in a new light. More importantly, the growing awareness of fundamental negative impacts undermines the explanatory force and legitimacy of the development paradigm itself – and thus the polarity between North and South. Problems such as hunger, climate change and all forms of structural violence can only be understood in a global context. The global expansion of the externalisation mechanism, through which the 'developed' early industrialised countries shift the social and environmental costs and risks of their development to other regions (in the 'South') and into the future, is reaching its limit. To the extent that distances across time and space are shrinking and truly global markets are emerging, it is becoming clear that the notion of 'outside' implied by 'externalisation' was always an illusion. Human beings and nature, whose exploitation was, and is, integral to the development of the North, no longer remain on the outside. The question of what we make of our life together for the benefit of all, and for the benefit of each and every generation (including those to come), can no longer be answered by a compass whose needle always points 'North'.

Nonetheless, differences remain between North and South – not only between the different ways people live, but also between their basic opportunities: their access to resources, the realisation of their human rights, their nutrition, health, education, life expectancy, security, and their political and economic participation. Moreover, these differences are amplified in the context of the rapid urbanisation that has accompanied globalisation, and that is transforming identities, life-styles and world-views.

That urbanisation is transforming our world is already evident in the statistics and is the focus of Messner's opening essay Humanity on the Move. In it Messner highlights how the 21st century will be the century of the cities and how the force of this urbanisation surge will primarily affect developing countries and emerging economies in Asia and Africa. Therefore, as Messner argues, if we are to address climate change and implement the 2030 Agenda, this can only be done in the context of new and different urban perspectives and strategies. Models of progress, resource consumption, forms of political association and governance, the nature of work, culture and pluralism are fundamentally transformed in this process of rapid and radical urbanisation. Theological and ethical reflection on the nature and impacts of this urbanisation is both essential and overdue.

In order to address this neglect, part two of this volume pursues a series of theological reflections on urbanisation and its challenges. Martin Ebner reflects on how the theme of cities has been present in Christian thought from its very beginnings and highlights how, in the time of Paul, the perception of city was transformed and replaced other operative motifs, including especially the Imperium Romanum. Margit Eckholt extends the theological reflection in the context of hospitality and shows how cities create new preconditions for the faith of its inhabitants and argues for a brave new way of working and living. By contrast, Felix Wilfred focuses in his farewell article regarding his presidency, not on the opportunities, but rather on the ambiguities of cities as public spaces. In a searing condemnation of neoliberalism's impact on the poor and marginalized, particularly in cities, Wilfred argues for a theological vision and agenda that pursues a humanistic vision of coexistence in cities, one that makes common cause with others in the pursuit of humane communities and ecologically sound habitats.

Wilfred's analysis is both theological and ethical, and part three turns its attention in a more focused manner to the ethical dimensions of urbanisation. Both Michelle Becka and Daniel Franklin Pilario frame their respective ethical reflections in the context of globalisation and the differentiated positions occupied by cities North and South, where the boundaries of these categories are increasingly blurred. Thus, Becka discusses global responsibility from the perspective of Germany (one of the engines of industrialisation and globalisation) while considering the conditions necessary for a just city. Pilario's point of departure is the globalised megacity of Manila. His focus is on the role of faith and religion therein, and particularly on the ability of religion to provide a vision of humane co-operation. Much like Wilfred, Pilario sees seeds of hope in the praxis of lived religion. Hogan's analysis also focuses on the issue of humane co-operation arguing that the cities have a crucial role to play in managing pluralism while also promoting social cohesion.

Following on from the theoretical perspectives, the fourth part foregrounds the praxis of creating humane spaces. The section consists of five inspiring cases of civil society actors who work to address the challenges in different geographical, policy and infrastructural contexts. Stephan De Beer's focus is that of post-apartheid cities, with their challenges of spatial (re)segregation, homelessness and precarious housing. His imperatives for theological action are drawn from his deep practical engagement with this issue. Georg Stoll meanwhile discusses how such trends re-focus the activities of NGOs like MISEREOR in global megacities, while Zárate discusses the inspirational work of the Habitat International Coalition which has been working for forty years to defend the rights of individuals to have a safe place to live with dignity and respect. Marco Kusumawijaya's perspective from Indonesia reflects on his role as an architect and urbanist and speaks to the challenges of creating an eco-social development. Luiz Kohara's essay completes the praxis-focus with a discussion of the role and impact of the NGO Centro Gaspar Garcia in São Paulo, which he co-founded, and which works for social inclusion amongst the most marginalised of the urban population.

Contrary to what has been long held, the world has not become a global village, rather it has become a global city. How this city continues to develop will depend not only on its diverse heritage and the existing structures and institutions, but also on how well people from the various continents succeed in exploring joint ways of living together, and in the process, creating new identities and solidarities that enable a good life for all.

Our issue concludes with an extended Forum essay that charts the recent change in the Catechism regarding the Catholic church's position on the death penalty. Presented by Michael Seewald the essay analyses the Catholic Church's position on the death penalty in its historical and theological dimensions. Moreover he highlights how Pope Francis' position represents a doctrinal innovation and concludes with a searching and provocative question about how this theological and doctrinal innovation on the death penalty coheres with the self-image of the magisterium of the Catholic church.

Markus Büker, Alina Krause, Linda Hogan

Part One: Humanity on the Move

The Century of Cities:
Pathways Towards Sustainability

DIRK MESSNER

The 21st century will be the century of the cities. Urban areas are becoming the central organizational form for almost all human societies. The global urban population could increase from just under 4 billion today to 7.5 billion people by 2050 – and urban infrastructures will grow with it. About two-thirds of humanity will then have their homes in cities. The force of the urbanization surge will primarily affect developing countries and emerging economies in Asia and Africa. Almost 90 % of urban-population growth up to 2050 is expected on these two continents (UN DESA, 2014). Nearly three quarters of the global urban population will then be living there (UN DESA, 2015). Climate change goals and the implementations of the 2030 Agenda can only be achieved based on fundamentally changed urban perspectives and strategies.

I Introduction

Humanity is on the move. This manifests itself in demographic growth within cities, as a result of the influx of people from the countryside to the city and from small and medium-sized towns to the metropolises; of migration both between poor countries and between poor and rich countries; and of social advancement from shanty towns to middle-class neighbourhoods. This relocation of humanity could become a process of social change that has most powerful impacts in the 21st century.

Urbanization has a formative effect on the world economy and society, on people's quality of life, on the future of democracy, as well as on the global consumption of resources and energy – and thus on the future of the Earth as a whole. Cities offer many opportunities for cultural, social

13

and economic development, and for improving resource and energy efficiency. But urbanization must be actively managed in order to counter the following risks: in developing countries and emerging economies, one third of the urban population do not have access to adequate housing; in sub-Saharan Africa, this figure is even higher at almost two thirds. In 2012 more than 850 million people were living in slums (UN DESA, 2015) without adequate access to vital infrastructures. How can the number of slum dwellers be prevented from doubling or even tripling? In sub-Saharan Africa, two-thirds of all new city-dwellers currently move into informal settlements or slums, and half of them are expected to remain there in the long term. According to UN forecasts, Africa's population could rise to a total of 4.4 billion people by 2100 (UN DESA, 2015). If the current urbanization trends were to continue in Africa, and, for example, 80 % of the people in Africa were to live in cities by 2100 – and 60 % of these in slums – this would mean about 2 billion people having to live in degrading city districts. Such a development must be prevented for reasons of social responsibility, but also from the perspective of security policy, since the massive social exclusion of people always carries with it the potential of societal destabilization.

A fundamental change of perspective is needed here, one that does not fight the symptoms but focuses on what causes the emergence of informal settlements with inadequate housing. In addition, what can be done to ensure that quality of life increases in cities, and people can make the most of their potential? What are the characteristics of cities worth living in? Cities and urban societies are responsible for the overwhelming majority of all worldwide resource consumption and greenhouse-gas emissions. How can the global urbanization surge be harnessed to ensure that efforts to improve quality of life are decoupled from environmental pollution – and that natural life-support systems are safeguarded? To achieve this, existing guiding concepts and strategies must be adapted (or new ones invented), developed and implemented. In view of the expected massive extension of the urban infrastructure, the challenge from the outset lies in avoiding path dependencies. If the new districts and cities were built according to the resource- and emissions-intensive models used in the last two centuries, global society would find itself in conflict with the planetary guard rails in the course of the 21st century. In other words, the spread of conventional urbanization on a global scale must be stopped.

II Urbanization and the Great Transformation towards Sustainability

The WBGU has already examined the topic of urbanization in the context of the 'Great Transformation' towards sustainability, which it analysed in its 2011 flagship report (WBGU, 2011). Now the WBGU applies the Great Transformation towards sustainability to urban areas (WBGU, 2016). WBGU's intention is to clarify where challenges and opportunities lie and to point out the areas where fundamental modifications and system changes are required.

Cities and their populations are drivers of global environmental change, while at the same time being affected by it. In this context, mitigation of climate change is one of the greatest challenges of the transformation: unabated climate change would jeopardize humankind's life-support systems. The extensive analyses conducted by the IPCC reveal the specific impact on cities. Many urban areas are situated in low-lying coastal zones, where there are particularly serious hazards – e.g. as a result of a combination of sea-level rise, the subsidence of land masses caused by the weight of buildings and groundwater depletion, storm events and flooding. Other risks are associated with the urban heat island effect, droughts and water scarcity. In order to achieve the target agreed at the UN climate conference in Paris in 2015 of holding the increase of global average temperature to well below 2 °C above pre-industrial levels, fossil CO_2 emissions should be completely stopped by 2070 – or correspondingly earlier if the more ambitious limitation of the increase to 1.5 °C is to be achieved. Consequently, the energy system in every city must also be decarbonized by that date. For this to happen, the dominance of the system of fossil-energy use must soon be overcome. Furthermore, both the mobility sector and systems for heating and cooling buildings will also have to get by without fossil CO_2 emissions in the future. There are encouraging signs that the international community is moving closer to this decisive turnaround. The public discourse on anthropogenic climate change has shifted significantly in just a few years and is now broadly anchored in society. The 2015 Paris Agreement is exemplary for the worldwide consensus on the need to mitigate anthropogenic climate change. Cities are the biggest consumers of energy and will thus play a key role in the implementation of the agreement.

The progress of the Great Transformation will depend substantially

15

on the decisions that will be taken in cities over the next few years and decades. There is a need for a paradigm shift away from incremental approaches that are essentially driven by short-term requirements, towards transformative changes with a strategic, long-term view of humanity's natural life-support systems and the creation of a form of urbanity that sustainably promotes human quality of life. In this context, it is not so important to look to the future from today's perspective, which usually makes the path already being followed look inevitable; rather, one should look back to the present from a desirable future: what paths should be followed and what dead-ends should be avoided today to make this sustainable future possible?

With this change of perspective, the WBGU places people, their quality of life, their capabilities and options for action, as well as their long-term future prospects, at the centre of its reflections on cities. There is a certain tradition in the idea that development concepts and strategies should be geared to people and their quality of life – and not only to growth prospects. Almost three decades ago, the United Nations Children's Emergency Fund (UNICEF, 1987) and the UN Economic Commission for Latin America and the Caribbean (UN CEPAL, 1996) were already calling for an economic "adjustment with a human face" in their criticism of the one-sidedly neoliberal structural-adjustment programmes of the World Bank and the International Monetary Fund. Securing a minimum of supplies and services (e.g. access to adequate housing, food, health, education) for all should be seen as a target system of development. This orientation can also be found in the Millennium Development Goals (MDGs) adopted in 2000. In the last few years, it has become clear that even when these minimum standards are met, significant sections of the population often do not participate at all, or not enough, in the process of economic and societal development. Poverty reduction does not guarantee that all people are equal before the law and will not suffer discrimination. So the aim must also be to reduce the considerable social and economic inequalities and to prevent the social, political and cultural marginalization and exclusion of – in some cases sizeable – sections of the population in urban societies. The Sustainable Development Goals (SDGs) internationally agreed in 2015 lay down a framework for this, particularly SDG no. 10: "Reduce inequality within and among countries" and SDG no. 11: "Make cities and human settlements inclusive, safe, resilient and sustainable".

Against this background, the WBGU, with its people-oriented view of urbanization, advocates a comprehensive concept of quality of life and prosperity which goes beyond minimum targets of substantive inclusion: e.g. overcoming absolute poverty and ensuring appropriate housing. It also contains comprehensive political and economic inclusion, i.e. the belief that the urban population should be enabled to take an active part in urban development. The WBGU's concept also aims to take into account essential preconditions for human quality of life, such as self-efficacy, identity, solidarity, a sense of belonging, trust and social networks. On the one hand, reversing the trends of growing inequality in people's living conditions and development opportunities, and realizing the transition from exclusion to inclusion are prerequisites and goals for human development; on the other hand, this is the only way in which risks for the stability of urban societies, nation states and ultimately also the global community of states can be contained. The current implosions and explosions of a rising number of societies in countries of north and sub-Saharan Africa, which are characterized by high levels of exclusion, are a warning signal to the international community that should not be overlooked. The WBGU has developed a 'normative compass' to help shaping the massive changes in the 'century of cities' in a people-oriented way. This compass comprises three dimensions:

- *First*, sustaining natural life-support systems by complying with planetary guard rails and protecting the local environment.
- *Second*, ensuring substantive, political and economic inclusion for the city dwellers.
- *Third*, the WBGU draws attention to the socio-cultural and spatial diversity of cities and urban societies, as well as the resulting plurality of urban transformation pathways: every city must seek 'its own way' to a sustainable future. This *Eigenart* (a German word meaning 'character') is not only hugely important for creating urban quality of life and identity, it is also an indispensable resource in the sense of developing each city's specific potential for creativity and innovation. With the dimension of *Eigenart*, the WBGU is introducing a new category into the sustainability discussion.

The WBGU advocates paying greater attention to polycentric approaches to urban development. The concentration of the population in one or a few central locations and urban agglomerations, which can be observed in many regions of the world, coupled with simultaneous economic, social, political and cultural marginalization and discrimination against rural and small-town areas, leads to (mega-)cities 'sucking in' more and more people, resources and capital at the expense of their surrounding areas. The influence of cities, which will expand on a global scale by the middle of the century, now extends from the direct hinterland to remote regions. Brenner et al. (2013) have described this reach of the urban demand for resources as 'planetary urbanization'.

Not infrequently, deserted, unattractive rural regions are left behind, while rapidly growing (mega-)cities emerge – especially in developing countries and emerging economies – with overtaxed infrastructures, overburdened municipal administrations, hostile-to-life settlement structures and socio-economically polarized urban societies. Thailand is an example. More than 80 % of Thailand's urban population live in the capital Bangkok (World Bank, 2015: 114). The WBGU recommends a change of direction. Polycentric approaches could make cities more attractive, avoid the disadvantages of excessive urban concentration and densification, and, at the same time, mobilize the advantages of decentralized settlement patterns. The conventional dichotomy between migration into and away from cities, and between the concentration and dispersion of settlement structures, is overcome by an approach which, instead of clearly separating 'city' from 'country' and 'centre' from 'periphery', systematically focuses on networking between poles of settlement and on the spaces in-between which connect small and large cities and rural areas.

Polycentric urban development is, for example, an EU policy framework and focuses on bridge-building between agglomeration and deconcentration, not on their polarization. By strengthening small and medium-sized towns and networking them with larger cities, it combines the advantages of agglomeration and decentralization.

Such a hybrid settlement strategy that emphasizes polycentric approaches is relevant for a number of dimensions in urban development.

• With *polycentric spatial structures* better use can be made of resources if water, food and energy no longer have to be transported over long distances into the few centres. Decentralized provision of renewable energies and digital networking can support the advantages of polycentric spatial structures.

• *Polycentric settlement structures* and polycentric cities promote the formation of cultural identity. They combine a diversity of urban societies with manageable settlement patterns and neighbourhoods, can restrict trends towards segregation, and open up spaces for connectivity and innovation.

• *Polycentric urban structures* increase the absorptive capacity and resilience of urban societies vis-à-vis shocks (such as climate-induced extreme events or waves of immigration).

• *Polycentric decision-making and polycentric governance structures* in cities promote the participation opportunities of local civil society and collaborative governance.

• Cities should furthermore be embedded in a *polycentric responsibility architecture*. Giving cities and their civil societies more creative freedom within their nation states to shape their development pathways (vertical embedding of the cities plus local scope for shaping and planning) and enabling them to network horizontally leads to the development of a governance and responsibility architecture that is tiered locally, nationally and globally. Here, responsibilities should be distributed among different, mutually (semi-)independent nodes over different levels of governance. This polycentric governance approach creates coordinating mechanisms and reflexivities that highlight the relative independence of cities (but also of nations), and a simultaneously high level of interdependence between them (Messner, 1997; Stichweh, 2004; Ostrom, 2010).

III A Normative Compass for the Transformation Towards a Sustainable 'World Cities Society'

The WBGU has developed a 'normative compass' to provide orientation for societal action in the light of the above requirements. It describes the constraints within which cities' development pathways towards a people-oriented form of urbanization should be realized, and which, if breached, would put sustainable development at risk.

The key message of the WBGU is that the transformation can be achieved by a combination of three dimensions:

• *Sustain natural life-support systems*: all cities should pursue development pathways that take account of the planetary guard rails

19

relating to global environmental change and solve local environmental problems to ensure sustainable urban development and the protection of the natural life-support systems. This involves, for example, meeting the 2 °C climate-protection guard rail and combating health-damaging air pollution; further examples include ending land and soil degradation and stopping the loss of phosphorus, an essential resource for agriculture.
• *Ensure inclusion*: universal minimum standards for substantive, political and economic inclusion should be met in all cities and by all cities. The aim here is to give all people access to human safety and development, enabling them to evolve and implement their individual and collective ways of living. In this sense, inclusion is simultaneously a means and an end. Substantive, political and economic inclusion mirrors many human rights that have already been internationally codified or discussed. Furthermore, such inclusion is based on the idea that people need corresponding opportunities to realize and implement these rights. *Substantive inclusion* lays the foundations: access e.g. to food, clean drinking water, sanitation, healthcare and education is the essential minimum standard for securing basic human needs. *Economic inclusion* entails, in particular, access to the labour and real-estate markets. When people are made the main focus, they must be granted electoral rights – as well as procedural rights of information and involvement – in order to achieve political inclusion and a right to judicial control. This ensures that any violation of these rights can be sanctioned.
• *Promote 'Eigenart'*: with the dimension of *Eigenart*, the WBGU is introducing a new category into the sustainability discussion. According to the WBGU's normative concept, the first two dimensions – sustaining the natural life-support systems and ensuring inclusion – open up a framework for a wide variety of transformation pathways. Within this framework, every urban society can and must pursue its individual course towards a sustainable future. On the one hand, *Eigenart* comprises all that is typical of each particular city. This can be described on the basis of its socio-spatial and constructed environment, its socio-cultural characteristics and local urban practices (descriptive *Eigenart*). On the other hand, *Eigenart* is a target or orientation dimension of urban transformations: it emphasizes that socio-cultural diversity in and of cities, their urban form, and the autonomy of city residents are key components of people-oriented urban transformation

in the creation of urban quality of life and identity (normative Eigenart). In this normative connotation of *Eigenart*, people are seen as actors who use their inclusion rights and thus design their cities in different and specific ways in order to realize quality of life. *Eigenart* thus enables and equips people to develop self-efficacy and to shape urban societies and urban spaces, in order to develop quality of life, trust, identity and a sense of belonging – and to design cities, infrastructures and spaces in a way that supports this. In the WBGU's view, two essential principles must be guaranteed to enable people and urban societies to develop *Eigenart* – and thus quality of life and sustainability: (1) the recognition of creative autonomy, i.e. that the residents themselves should shape and appropriate urban spaces, and (2) the recognition of difference, i.e. the recognition of the Diversity of Cultural Expressions (UNESCO, 1997) and the individual opportunity to appropriate cultural identities. The introduction of the concept of Eigenart draws attention to the spatial-social pre-requisites for the appropriation of space, and thus for the creation of urban quality of life, social cohesion and local identity. It also makes it possible to take account of the diversity of cities and their transformation pathways. The spotlight is thus directed at the many and varied forms, designs and cultural manifestations of urban areas. The focus is also on the specific potential for social and economic creativity and innovation which develops as a result of local interactions (connectivity) between stakeholders from different societal spheres. Furthermore, the WBGU regards diversity in and of cities as an important resource for the urban transformation towards sustainability.

Cities should take their orientation from universal sustainability and inclusion goals, but keep their *Eigenart*. Universal inclusion rights, as described above, are a necessary prerequisite for people and urban societies to draft and manage their own development pathways – universal inclusion rights and the Eigenart of the cities are mutually dependent and generate interactions.

Complying with planetary ecological guard rails and ensuring substantive, political and economic inclusion represent global minimum standards for the 21st century's civilizatory project for humankind. As concepts, '*sustainable development*' and '*inclusion*' each contain a dialectical principle. In the case of sustainable development, the principle is the need to find a balance between conservation on the one hand, and, on the other, the facilitation of development, which historically is associated with 'growth', i.e. with 'having more and consuming more'. In the case of inclusion, it is the balance between the collective idea of 'sharing' and that of individual 'having' that needs to be found. Against this background, *Eigenart* becomes both a normative orientation and a source of innovative strength for a humanity on the move. The German word *Eigenart* (which means 'character', or more literally 'own way' or 'own type/kind') is itself characterized by the dialectic of *Eigen* ('own', i.e. individual, new, different, distinctive) and *Art* ('way' or 'type/kind'), as an expression of class, community, group, generalizability.

Sustainable, future-oriented societal development and quality of life can only evolve if these dialectics and tensions are balanced out in situations of dynamic equilibrium. Concepts of society that aim to overcome this dialectical complexity and the seemingly paradoxical contradictions of societal development – as expressed in the terms 'sustainable development', 'inclusion' and '*Eigenart*' – by propagating narrow-minded imperatives for unlimited growth or the primacy of the 'individual' or 'society'/'community' – are destined to fail. This applies to the radical capitalist concepts of the 'shareholder society' and to Milton Friedman's view that there are no societies, but only individuals; it also applies to community protagonists of right-wing, left-wing, and sometimes even religious provenance, where the rights of individuals are made subordinate to the 'greater whole'. The urban transformation towards sustainability can only succeed if transformation pathways are developed which balance out the ambiguity, dialectic and tensions expressed in the terms 'sustainable development', 'inclusion' and '*Eigenart*'.

Based on the interaction between the dimensions of sustaining the natural life-support systems, inclusion and *Eigenart*, the WBGU provides a compass for dealing with fundamental upheavals in the century of urbanization. With its normative compass for sustainable urban development, the WBGU tries to take the global diversity of cities into account.

Notes

1. This article is based on a report of the German Advisory Council of Global Change: WBGU (2016): *Humanity on the Move – Unlocking the transformative power of cities*, Berlin: WBGU

Bibliography

Brenner, N. (ed.) (2014) *Implosions/Explosions. Towards a Study of Planetary Urbanization.* (Berlin: Jovis Verlag)

Messner, D. (1997) *The Network Society*, (London: Frank Cass Publishers)

Ostrom, E. (2010) 'Polycentric Systems for Coping with Collective Action and Global Environmental Change', *Global Environmental Change* 20, 550–557.

Stichweh, R. (2004), Der Zusammenhalt der Weltgesellschaft: Nicht-normative Integrationstheorien in der Soziologie' in Beckert, J., Eckert, J., Kohli, M. and Streeck, W. (eds.) *Transnationale Solidarität. Chancen und Grenzen*, (Frankfurt/M., New York: Campus) 236-245.

UN CEPAL – United Nations Comisión Económica para América Latina y el Caribe (1996) *Transformación Productiva con Equidad. La Tarea Prioritaria del Desarrollo de América Latina y el Caribe en los Años Noventa.* (Santiago: CEPAL)

UN DESA – United Nations Department of Economic and Social Affairs (2014) *World Urbanization Prospects. The 2014 Revision. Highlights.* ST/ESA/SER.A/352. (New York: UN DESA)

UN DESA – United Nations Department of Economic and Social Affairs (2015) *World Urbanization Prospects. The 2014 Revision. Final Report.* ST/ESA/SER.A/366. (New York: UN DESA)

UNESCO – United Nations Educational, Scientific and Cultural Organization (1997) *Our Creative Diversity. Report of the World Commission on Culture and Development* (Pérez de Cuéllar-Report) (Paris: UNESCO)

UN-Habitat – United Nations Human Settlements Programme (2011) *Global Report on Human Settlements 2011: Cities and Climate Change* (Nairobi: UN-Habitat)

UNICEF – United Nations Children's Fund (1987) *Annual Report 1987* (New York: UNICEF)

WBGU – German Advisory Council on Global Change (2011) *World in Transition – A Social Contract for Sustainability. Flagship Report* (Berlin: WBGU)

WBGU – German Advisory Council on Global Change (2016) *Humanity on the Move. The Transformative Power of Cities*, (Berlin: WBGU)

World Bank (2015) *East Asia's Changing Urban Landscape: Measuring a Decade of Spatial Growth* (Washington, DC: World Bank)

Christians as Troublemakers in the City: Initial Experiences and Visions On the Value of Christian Faith for Shaping Society

MARTIN EBNER

The shaping of what we today call 'Christianity' took place in the great cities of the Roman Empire. Considering it against this background highlights the particular features of this beginning. This article explores them with the aid of the Pauline letters and the architecture of the City of God described in Revelation 21ff.

Christianity grew to adulthood in the city.[1] The first places in which we can be certain that believers in Christ lived are cities, indeed urban centres of the Roman Empire: Corinth, Ephesus, Damascus, Antioch – and finally Rome itself. And moreover Christians were responsible for disorder in these cities, giving offence within the Jewish synagogue communities because of their lax attitude to the conditions for joining the holy people of God, and even being subversive in the wider city because within their own ranks they experimented with alternative models of society, at least in the Pauline communities. And it was none other than Paul, with his upbringing as a Pharisee – before his dramatic switch – who discovered these dissidents in Damascus (Acts 9), and at first tried to eliminate them (Gal 1.13), but then developed and theologically underpinned what had originally shocked him so much. What had seemed threatening to Paul and the synagogue communities, and yet at the same time represented the characteristic emphasis of the mission of the earliest believers in

Christ, was their willingness to open God's covenant to people who were interested in the monotheistic faith and Jewish ethics, 'God-fearers', as they were called, but shrank from circumcision and the dietary laws, because both were disapproved of in the Greco-Roman world.[2] Full membership was therefore denied to them in the synagogue communities, but not by the believers in Christ. This gave rise to sharp clashes in Jewish circles. Under Emperor Claudius in AD 49, Jewish trouble-makers were expelled from Rome (cf Suetonius, *Claudius*, 25.4), as can be seen from the fate of Prisca and Aquila (Acts 18.2), who were Jewish Christian missionaries who promoted and practised a 'Judaism light'. In Antioch, where the 'Gospel of Jesus as Lord' was also preached to the 'Greeks', the 'disciples' were for the first time officially listed as 'Christians' (Acts 11.20, 26),[3] in other words as an independent group alongside and outside the Jewish synagogue. This may have been the work of the Jewish leaders, who wanted to distinguish themselves from these dissidents, because their blurring of the Jewish identity markers might threaten the privileges enjoyed by 'the Jews'.

Baptism and the abolition of legally inspired divisions
It was probably also from these groups of Christian believers in Damascus and Antioch that Paul learned the baptismal tradition that he himself later quotes in his letters: 'As many of you as were baptised into Christ have clothed yourselves with Christ. There is no longer Jew or Greek, there is no longer slave or free, there is no longer male and female; for all of you are one in Christ Jesus' (Gal 3.27-28; cf 1 Cor 12.13). This abolished divisions, typical both of mainstream Judaism and of Greco-Roman society, that were the basis of hierarchies and helped to stabilise group identity. The fact that people dared to cross these boundaries as part of their normal practice – as almost an empirically perceptible splash of the colour of the new world (cf 2 Cor 5.17; Gal 6.15) - is the key sign of faith in Christ. Paul, a 'convert' also to this way of thinking, included clear signs of this change in his letters. He enthusiastically campaigned for the recognition of those Christian believers who were socially 'unequal', for the baptised slave Onesimus (in Philemon), against the propagandists of the idea that circumcision was necessary to complete baptism (Galatians), against the 'unworthy' celebration of the Lord's supper in Corinth, where the hosts made others aware of their inferior status *at the meal*. To be served different food according to one's rank and status was standard

practice in Greco-Roman culture, but if it happens among the baptised that makes the occasion simply a normal supper, but not the Lord's supper (1 Cor 11.17-34). For Paul the tangible recognition of those of the baptised who were of lower social status as in fact equals is the distinctive mark of Christianity.

The *ekklesiai* of God and the citizenship of the baptised

'*Ekklesiai* of God' is the name Paul gives to these groups whose Christian faith enables them to transcend the divisions of the Old World. To people living in cities, this term would call to mind the citizen assemblies that discussed city affairs and took decisions by a vote. It should be noted that only freeborn men could attend these assemblies and vote – no women, no slaves, no men without the citizenship that was passed down from generation to generation in old-established families. Believers in Christ thought of themselves by analogy as God's citizen assemblies, but with different membership criteria (faith in Christ) and a different composition (they included women, female and male slaves and non-citizens). All these had the right to exercise the citizenship of the baptised. They formed regulated *ekklesiai* (Rom 16.23; 1 Cor 11.18, 20; 14.23); their rules gave women and men an equal right to speak (1 Cor 11.4-5).[4] Difficult decisions, even about individuals, were taken by a show of hands (2 Cor 2.6; 8.19). Under Roman rule the autonomy of the *ekklesiai* in the cities had shrivelled to almost nothing.[5] Paul is almost reviving an old constitutional right of cities and transferring it to the groups of believers in Christ – though with modified membership criteria.

Christ's domains and subversive infiltration of Roman imperial structures

In Paul's thinking we can even detect a sort of strategic concept of mission that tries to infiltrate the structures of Roman rule in a targeted way and simply 'conquer' the world for Christ. The cities in which Paul founds communities or in which he spends a longer period of time are all colonies (that is, settlements of Roman veterans), such as Philippi, or capitals of provinces of the Roman empire (Thessalonica, Corinth, Ephesus). In other words, they are hubs from which the huge empire is 'ruled'. Each is the base of the local governor, who, with a small staff, holds the reins of power: foreign policy, jurisdiction including the death penalty – and finance, i.e. collecting taxes. In restive provinces Roman legions applied appropriate pressure. Paul did not just target these hubs of Roman rule; he even thought like the emperor. When 'the household of Stephanas' in Corinth were baptised, Paul identifies them as 'the first fruits (*aparche*) of (the province of) Achaia' (1 Cor 16.15). From Ephesus he writes: 'The *ekklesiai* of (the province of) Asia greet you' (1 Cor 16.19). According to 1 Thess 1.8, 'the word of the Lord has sounded forth from you' into the provinces of Macedonia and Achaia (cf also Rom 15.19, 26). In each case he is talking about the small house communities in Corinth and Ephesus, which probably numbered not many more than 30 to 40 members, probably fewer.[6] For Paul, however, they represent the new power that is subversively undermining Roman rule. If the Romans are conquering the world with their legions in order to subject it to their rule, that is, to exploit it financially, Paul wants to conquer the world with his gospel in order to subject it to the rule of Christ[7] – with the corresponding consequences for the social structuring of these new dominions of Christ, which together form a new network of communion.

The architecture of the City of God and the real utopias of Christianity
In the last work of the New Testament canon readers are allowed sight in a vision of the very architecture of the alternative city itself, the city of God as it comes down from heaven to earth (Rev 21.1-22.5). Its architecture gives us an insight into the conception of the alternative society intended by God. As is usual with descriptions of cities in the ancient world, readers are given a detailed description only of what they are meant to notice and what is meant to impress them. To put it another way, the gaps are crucial to discovering how the reader's gaze is being steered. In addition, in most cases an understanding of the Jewish background is necessary to decode the hidden messages, though this can be taken for granted as regards the intended readers.[8]

Multi-ethnic character
In terms of its layout the city of God is a Jewish city: with twelve gates named after the twelve tribes of Israel (cf Ezek 48.30-34), a theme continued with the names of the twelve apostles of the Lamb inscribed on the foundation stones of the walls. But it is open for God's peoples (λαοί), in the plural (Rev 21.3; cf 5.9; 7.9), in other words, for all people who are not excluded under the terms of the two vice catalogues of Rev 21.8, 27, that is, those who have kept clear of the tendencies to assimilate to the

imperial power, Rome, as they were propagated among their own ranks (Nicolaitans, the prophetess Isabel).[9] They are written in the 'book of life' (Rev 21.27), by analogy with the corresponding citizen lists of the cities, full citizens of the city of God, thus giving the city, behind its traditional Jewish exterior, a multi-ethnic stamp.

The blood supply for the inhabitants

Normally Greek cities display a grid pattern of streets, with right-angled intersections, into which the temple, public buildings and squares are integrated. The typical Roman city layout has two main thoroughfares, the *cardo* and the *decumanus*, which are markedly wider than all the other streets and set apart from them architecturally by colonnades on either side. In principle they divide the city into four equal parts, though sometimes they have to fit the geographical features of the site, but their intersection always brings one to the forum, where the capitol and possibly the temple of Caesar and the basilica represent the Roman central administration in both religious symbolism and practical effect. The street plan of the city of God, in contrast, which the reader can easily imagine by remembering the three gates on each side, clearly breaks with this pattern: the three times three main streets which cut through the city divide it into a total of 16 districts. They do not lead to an architecturally imposing centre of power,[10] but are 'arteries' for the inhabitants. Instead of colonnades, behind which the city's most select shops display their wares, they are lined with fruit trees.[11] The fruit and the medicinal leaves are freely available to all the inhabitants. The trees are planted along a stream of crystal clear water – quite different from the situation in many towns under Roman administration, in which a foul sewer beside the main street filled the air with its stench (Pliny the Younger, *Letters* X.98).

An alternative city

When considering the appearance of a city, ancient authors focused on the size and area. In order to get higher figures, Pliny the Elder, to take one example, calculates the size of Rome by taking the length of all the streets, which would give a total of more than 60 miles, and if the height of the buildings were also included, no city in the world would surpass Rome in size (*Natural History*, 3.67). The lengths of the streets of the new Jerusalem also steadily increase from Ezekiel 46, via the plans in the Qumran texts to the Sibylline Oracles (5.252), according to which the walls of the new Jerusalem stretch as far as Jaffa on the sea. A normal city such as Timgad in North Africa was about 1,100 x 1,200 ft (around 335 m) wide. In contrast, the square City of God measures 12,000 stadia, about 2,200 km, on each side. This not only gives it an area of around 5 million sq. km, but means that, when it comes down from heaven to earth, it covers the entire Roman empire.[12] In other words, the city of refuge expected by believers in Christ and open to all who rejected assimilation, replaces the *imperium romanum* claimed by the Romans.

The city as the Holy of Holies

The city is also 2,200 km high (cf Rev 21.16), which makes it a totally surreal cubic city. This makes the City of God not only unrivalled down to the present, but also – considered in Jewish terms – a huge provocation. The cube form is reserved to the Holy of Holies in the temple (cf 1 Kings 6.20; 2 Chr 3.8; cf Ezek 41.4), which only the high priest is allowed to enter, and then only once a year and with the most extreme liturgical security measures (Lev 16.12-17). It now becomes clear why there is no temple in the city (Rev 22.1): the city itself *is* the temple's Holy of Holies.*13* And all the citizens of this city move around within this space. We could also put it this way: the City of God as described in Rev 21-22 is a city without a centre of worship, but full of priestly people in God's presence. Now if we know that the whole Jerusalem temple area was divided into hierarchically determined areas of access (from the court of the gentiles, which was strictly separated from the Jewish area, which in its turn leads into the women's court, then into the men's court and then into court of the priests, who alone are allowed to enter the altar area and the outside parts of the temple, while only the high priest is allowed, once a year, to enter the Holy of Holies), and if we know that – according to the account of the Jewish historian and priest Josephus (*Life* 1) – in Judaism membership of the priesthood denotes nobility or prominence in a family, we can understand how explosive this conception is in socio-political terms. All 'citizens' of the City of God are – as befits citizens – of equal status and also 'nobles': as priests before God, irrespective of the rank they were born into or the ethnic group from which they come.[14] The analogy with Gal 3.28 is startling.[15]

A social utopia

The City of God is built of materials out of which the great merchants had made their fortunes out of trade with Rome's elites: gold, precious stones and pearls (cf Rev 21.18-21). They burst into tears at the fall of the 'whore Babylon', because they have lost their market (cf Rev 18.11-16). Understood in this internal context, this image of the most precious materials out of which the ideal city in the vision is built, itself taken from utopian description of cities, continues the socio-political theme. In the City of God the things that enrich the political and economic elite in the Roman world become accessible to all inhabitants: all walk along streets of pure gold, all live within walls of precious stones and gates of pearls (Rev 21.18,21). And if we remember that in the Roman world it is the census, the estimate of personal wealth, which determines entry into the group of the *honestiores*, the higher classes of the *decuriones*, knights and senators, we see that in the City of God the basis for these distinctions is removed.

A political utopia
The 'citizens' of the city are both slaves and kings (Rev 22.2-5). The first relationship exists with God, before whom all are always slaves, while kingship belongs to the status of 'citizens' of the City of God, in which the kingdom of God becomes a reality because the only people who have access to it are those who live according to God's will (cf Rev 21.8,27). Since there is neither a religious nor a social hierarchy among the inhabitants, all will 'reign as kings' (βασιλεύσουσιν), though they will have no subjects. All have the status of rulers but the act of ruling is reduced to absurdity. The 'royal power' of God's 'slaves' consists in the worship of God (λατρεύσουσιν), as is to be expected of people who are (high) priests. Here the sociology of the City of God adopts the connection between the political and the sacred realms in the forum that was typical of the architecture of Roman cities, but gives it a new connotation. The two sides of the demonstration of Roman power to the people of the city are transposed into the definition of the status of the people in the city: they are both priests and kings – provided that they give God the glory.

To sum up, the description of the City of God in Revelation 21-22 details the kingdom of God (βασιλεία τοῦ θεοῦ) as a city that replaces the *Imperium Romanum*, that is, the kingdom of the Romans. In doing so it takes the traditional biblical imagery of God's royal power, which in practice was based on the imagery of oriental or Hellenistic monarchies, and transposes it to the imaginative world of city culture. From this position it produces a provocative critique both of Rome's power structure, which had only avoided the term 'monarchy', and of the social order established by Rome. Through the description of architecture and social interactions Revelation 21-22 implies a change in the structure of society that is wholly in accord with Gal 3.28.

Looking ahead

Christianity grew to maturity in the city, and it almost seems as though the survival of Christianity will be decided in the great conurbations of the 21st century. The visions the New Testament writings offer us for this prospect, and the directions believers in Christ in fact took in the 1st century, are far from having outlived their usefulness. Described in relation to their roots in the culture of their time, they give us expressive analogies for today. And what they show is that the real scandal the first Christian communities created was that they understood the exaltation of the Crucified One to be joint ruler with God as the task of living here and *now in this world* under *his* rule as *his* citizens, in other words to make a start on relevant social changes in their own ranks and reject any sort of cooperation that conflicted with this goal. They realised that anyone who did not start practising this new way of life here and now would not be able to enter the City of God that God had already planned, and which was coming down *to the earth*. In short, for the first believers in Christ practising the faith in the God who raises the dead meant reshaping everyday social environments. Theocentricity taken seriously cannot put up with hierarchies constructed by human beings, different levels of social and religious rank. The decision is coming in the cities....

Translated by Francis McDonagh

Notes

1. For a detailed account see Martin Ebner, 'Die Stadt als Lebensraum der ersten Christen', *Das Urchristentum in seiner Umwelt* I (GNT 1,1), Göttingen, 2012.

2. A penis not concealed by a foreskin, that is the exposed head, was associated with permanent sexual excitation; cf Andreas Blaschke, 'Beschneidung. Zeugnisse der Bibel und verwandter Texte' (TANZ 28), Tübingen 1998; constantly to refuse pork would inevitably provoke suspicion and also be regarded as unreasonable, since pork was regarded, particularly by the Stoics, as particularly healthy.

3. χρηματίζειν/*chrematizein* is Roman official terminology. 'Christians' is a Latinising coinage and describes the supporters of a person; cf Hans G. Kippenberg, *Die vorderasiatischen Erlösungsreligionen in ihrem Zusammenhang mit der antiken Stadtherrschaft* (Stw 917), Frankfurt am Main, 1991, pp 300-301.

4. In phrasing that is completely parallel, we are told here that both men and women 'speak and prophesy' – only hairstyle must be gender-specific! The instruction that women should be silent in the *ekklesia* (cf 1 Cor 14.34-35) is in all probability a post-Pauline interpolation (cf 1 Tim 2 11-12).

5. Their main function was to vote marks of recognition for the deserving.

6. Cf John S. Kloppenborg, 'Membership Practices in Pauline Christ Groups', *Early Christianity* 4 (2013), 183–215, 189–195.

7. In 2 Cor 2.14-16 Paul refers to the Roman triumphal processions, held to celebrate a general's conquest of territory, to emphasise Christ's status as a conqueror, leading Paul with him to demonstrate 'the fragrance that comes from knowing' Christ (through Paul's preaching).

8. On the cultural background of the author and his readers, cf. Stefan Schreiber, 'Die Offenbarung des Johannes', M. Ebner and S. Schreiber (ed.), *Einleitung in das Neue Testament* (KStTh 6), Stuttgart, 2nd ed., 2013, pp 566–593, 573–576.

9. Cf Heinz Giesen, *Die Offenbarung des Johannes (Regensburger Neues Testament)*, Regensburg, 1997, pp 459-60, 472-73.

10. Nothing of the sort is ever mentioned. The location of God's throne (Rev 22.1) is never mentioned, but only its function: it is the source of the river of paradise.

11. Like ξύλον/'tree' in the sense of a number of trees (cf Giesen, *Die Offenbarung des Johannes*, p. 474), πλατεῖα in Rev 22,2, should be understood as 'streets' in general.

12. Certainly on its eastern side: calculated from Jerusalem, the imperial capital, Rome, is definitely covered.

13. Correspondingly, the wall of the city is referred to in Rev 20.16 by the same term (ἐνδώμησις), as used in inscriptions from Smyrna and Tralles, which are part of the immediately surrounding cultural environment, for the enclosure of a temple; cf Giesen, *Die Offenbarung des Johannes*, p. 467).

14. The status of priest in judaism was rooted in genealogy.

15. Even if women are not specifically mentioned, they are included in the 'priestly people' of the City of God.

Learning to Live a Life of Hospitality: Theological Foundations for Proclaiming the Faith in the Cultural Plurality of Big Cities

MARGIT ECKHOLT

Pope Francis regards 'pastoral conversion' as central to city ministry. The key to the proclamation of the faith is provided by the cities themselves and the processes of social, cultural and religious transformation taking place in them. A key concept of city ministry in this connection is 'hospitality'.

I Introduction: Faith in the 'new cultures' of big cities

Since the 1980s an intercontinental network focused on pastoral urbana or city ministry[1] – with which Pope Francis in his time as archbishop of Buenos Aires was connected –[2] has been thinking about emerging forms of faith and Church practice in the fast-moving spaces of metropolitan centres and mega-cities. In his Apostolic Exhortation *Evangelii Gaudium* Pope Francis draws attention to the 'new cultures' emerging in these spaces, driven by the energy, creativity and liveliness of changed forms of relationships and work, a product indeed of new communications media and a new 'style' of communal life, but driven also by the violence and fragility of precarious economic and social networks in the abysses and 'non-places' of big cities. 'New cultures are constantly being born in these vast new expanses where Christians are no longer the customary interpreters or generators of meaning. Instead, they themselves take from these cultures new languages, symbols, messages and paradigms which propose new approaches to life, approaches often in contrast with the

Gospel of Jesus. A completely new culture has come to life and continues to grow in the cities' (EG 73). This is where the Church has to be: 'It must reach the places where new narratives and paradigms are being formed, bringing the word of Jesus to the inmost soul of our cities' (EG 74).

In the following remarks I should like to outline the theological and ecclesiological framework for the changes that Pope Francis mentioned in *Evangelii Gaudium*. Evangelization means reaching 'the inmost soul of our cities', and this is only possible when the radical nature of the changes in our ways of life, and our religious life, in the fast-moving spaces of our cities on a cultural level are taken seriously. Studies in the sociology of religion indicate the breakdown of institutional ties to the Church. This is happening not just in European countries, but, because of the crisis of credibility that the Catholic Church has been suffering through the revelations of abuse and the misuse of power, in the countries of Latin America as well. Rejection of the Catholic Church as an institution, secularisation and the growth of religious pluralism – which in Latin America means the growth of Pentecostal churches and other charismatic forms of religious movement – are a feature of the breakdown of traditional forms of religion, and this is particularly intense in the mega-cities and large conurbations because of the dynamism, fascination and fragility of life in these turbulent spaces. This has turned cities into what the bishops at Aparecida called 'laboratories of this complex and many-sided contemporary culture' (509). The bishops produced an important and quite critical self-appraisal of the way they had dealt with the challenges created for the Catholic Church and its mission of evangelization by the cultural, social, political and religious transformations of our time. They talk about 'other religious groups' – and no longer, as they were still doing at the Latin American bishops' conferences in Puebla (1979) or Santo Domingo (1992), of the 'sects'[3] – and recognised that Catholics were turning to them, 'not for doctrinal but for experiential reasons…, not for strictly dogmatic, but for pastoral reasons; not due to theological problems, but to methodological problems of our Church. They hope to find answers to their concerns.'[4] There have now been very many studies, especially sociological studies, of the Pentecostal movement, and what they say is that these new churches are better able to find their place in the turbulent spaces of the cities and find it easier to react to cultural change.[5] In an interview at the end of the 2013 World Youth Day in Rio de Janeiro,[6] Pope Francis talked about the need for new ecumenical encounters and a different attitude to the charismatic movement within Catholicism,

36

and called for a 'pastoral conversion' and a related 'ecclesial conversion'. This is the overarching perspective of the Latin American network known as *pastoral urbana* (urban ministry), as it is of the research carried out in 2010-2014 by the project of the same name commissioned by the German bishops' conference.[7] When the character of evangelization is no longer decided by the Church, but determined in the light of the challenges posed by the city, as the theological and pastoral studies on *pastoral urbana* suggest, this means a return to the ecclesiological paradigm shift produced by the Second Vatican Council and its application to this new situation; it takes as its starting point the gospel of Jesus Christ, which becomes incarnate afresh in different cultural settings. I shall discuss this in more detail in the next section and then focus on the overall perspective of this 'ecclesial conversion' in the third and final section with a reference to the concept of hospitality as explored in modern French philosophy. 'Learning to live a life of hospitality' is the path an 'outgoing Church' must take, a new way of being a Christian and becoming the Church. It sets out with the energy of a constantly new departure, on a journey with so many others – other Christian denominations, other religions and all people of 'goodwill' and in the turbulent spaces of the city reveals the 'city of God' symbolically – sacramentally – by working for peace, justice and the defence of our common home, creation.

II 'Ecclesial conversion' – foundations for ecclesiology in the light of Vatican II and the Medellín conference

The relationship between Lumen Gentium and Gaudium et Spes
For the Catholic Church the Second Vatican Council meant an ecclesiological and theological paradigm shift, turning it from a Western Church into a world Church, from a hierarchically structured 'perfect society' to a Church as the people of God that acquires its specific expression among the variety of forms cultures offer, and shows itself to be the 'sacrament' of Jesus Christ especially when it is at the service of peace and justice and the developing unity of the one human race. The celebration of the 50th anniversary of the Latin American bishops' meeting in Medellín in 1968 reminded us of the significance of the Vatican II Pastoral Constitution *Gaudium et Spes* for this ecclesiological paradigm shift. With its 'option for the poor' the Latin American Church has radicalised the 'discovery of the world' that took place at Vatican II. 'Incarnation' into the world became

an abandonment of status in which the original meaning of the gospel was rediscovered, and it took on new expressions in the most diverse forms of action on the side of the poor and excluded, to the point of martyrdom, surrendering one's life. The laity now became leaders, a core feature of this new type of Church expressed in the idea of the people of God and *Lumen Gentium*'s emphasis on charisms, and their role is always particular, related to cultural, social, political and economic contexts. This role is an expression of Christian freedom, which comes to fulfilment as freedom in the recognition of the freedom of others, which means working for the liberation of the 'poor' and their chance to become leaders – and 'poor' here means all those who are excluded, whose rights and life prospects have been stolen from them, especially indigenous peoples, girls and women. When Pope Francis in *Evangelii Gaudium* talks about the 'new cultures' that are emerging in the cities, these cultures are the product of the creative and intertwined processes initiated by these new leaders; we have to recognise and understand them if we are to bring the gospel to the 'soul' of these new cultures.

Freedom and liberation in Jesus Christ

The basis of this recognition of others is the gaining of freedom in Jesus Christ. New forms of city ministry have to bear in mind this Christian freedom, which belongs to the essence of the Church, and use it to find the power to invent new, liberating forms of participation and communication in a Church 'in' the city. Contributing to an 'ecclesiogenesis', enabling the Church to be born, is only possible if all participate and if their diversity is recognised. The Second Vatican Council laid the foundation for this. It proclaimed an empowerment of all based on baptism, which summons all, men and women, young and old, to take responsibility for making their contribution to the construction of the people of God.[8] This includes allowing faith to be shaped by life, it includes educational processes, and an introduction to spirituality and piety. Of course it is important that the Church's liturgy and its services remain 'attractive', but the traditional 'Church of ritual' must open up so that new forms of participation and shared responsibility can emerge, a new relationship between priests and laity, men and women. As part of the research project on *pastoral urbana* the members of the women's theology association Teologanda from Buenos Aires have emphasised the importance of the role of education in the creation of living faith communities,[9] of the recognition of the abilities

38

of all, especially women, and the importance of new thinking about authority and the official structures of the Church. The Catholic Church cannot put off this renewal, in itself a sort of 'ecclesiogenesis', especially if in its service of the gospel it wants to reach the various emerging cultures. The Church is not 'apart from' the world; it takes its identity from the many lives people lead, and that is expressed in its liturgy, its rituals and official structures. These things are part of its contribution to the formation of citizenship, and that is also a pastoral task. The city of God and the human city are not alongside each other or opposite each other. No, in Jesus Christ God takes up residence in the human city and by so doing gives it an energy that breaks open all its narrowness and self-obsession – that of society, culture and Church too – and opens it up to the expanse of a God who is always greater, a space that leads to a new-look citizenship, centred on friendship with God and between human beings, based on the principle that 'There is no longer Jew or Greek, there is no longer slave or free, there is no longer male and female; for all of you are one in Christ Jesus' (Gal 3.28). In this way Christians become 'leaven' for this one world. They are not 'citizens of two worlds'; the 'city of God' grows in the 'human city'.

A new 'public theology' in the fast-moving space of the city
The multi-layered novelties of the 'fast-moving space of the city' to which Church ministry must respond has as yet hardly made itself felt in theological discussion, especially not in dogmatic theology. In contrast, in recent years the city has become a key topic in the human sciences, precisely because it reflects new developments in today's culture. The 'topographical' or 'spatial' shift in human sciences, developed to its greatest extent in interdisciplinary dialogue with human geography, approaches the city through the paradigm of space.[10] Spaces and places, borders and bridges, connecting lines, highways and light rail, all are important to describe a city. In the city's space cultures recreate themselves, in encounters, in the various 'translations', in the 'border areas'. The city is a 'fast-moving space',[11] in which cultures are not translated but take shape in mutual translation processes.[12] Theology for its part has tended to neglect this environment, even though it was precisely in the city that theology emerged as an academic discipline and developed a form of reasoned argument that presupposed universal structures of plausibility which transcended the contexts of science and culture. It was in the 'fast-moving city' of our time, above all, and facing what was for the Christian faith a

new situation of a fragmented, multi-religious and secular environment, that theology was questioned and challenged in a new way. Recognition of others, the autonomy of different areas of culture, freedom of conscience and religion, led theology to position itself in a different way in the 'fast-moving' city of our time. This means a de-centring of the ecclesiological perspective, but a new presence of the Christian faith 'among the nations'. Christians form the 'messianic people' among the nations; they are one actor among many in the culture, and their delivery of the gospel 'in the city' is what decides their 'profile'. This does not mean 'mission' in the traditional sense, but the realisation that the proclamation of the gospel grows in dialogue with many others, and is even 'present' among the others, precisely because the One whom Christians 'proclaim' is already there. The 'arrival city' is becoming the new locus of reference for the universality of the faith. Theology cannot be anything other than 'local'; it grows out of the various locales in this city in which theologians are at work. As 'local' theology, it is plural and 'in movement', just as the city is in movement. The theologian, man or woman, is constantly switching between different places in the city, and his or her theology grows 'in translation', is 'inter-cultural'. Life forms of the faith develop in the 'fast-moving space' of the city in tension-filled and creative plurality. These are Church places, in terms of which the theologian meditates on the new proclamation of the faith. What is proclaimed is always a new 'translation exercise' and in the complex processes of translation in which links are formed in the fragile, plural, tension-filled 'arrival city' theology is in the service of a Church that wants to be the 'sacrament of the nations'.[13] In the space of the 'arrival city' theology takes shape 'in translation' and it is in this process that it makes its contribution to 'pastoral conversion' or 'ecclesial conversion'.

III Hospitality in the 'arrival city'

In the political philosophy of recent decades the concept of 'hospitality' has been developed as a concept for exploring new forms of relationships with strangers and 'new arrivals' in a world that is becoming steadily smaller. Whereas Aristotle in his political philosophy regards hospitality as an imperfect form of friendship, because its object is merely 'benefit',[14] in Immanuel Kant's *Toward Perpetual Peace*, precisely because of the 'inhospitable behaviour of the civilised states in our part of the world, especially the commercial ones',[15] hospitality acquires a new significance. Kant defines hospitality as 'the right of a stranger not to be treated in a hostile manner by another upon his arrival in the other's territory'.[16] He 'develops the ancient idea of cosmopolitanism or world citizenship by recognising, for the first time, the right of a stranger to hospitality, thereby going beyond an ethics of humanity to argue for legal and political duties. The fact that Kant recognises the stranger as a subject, and above all a subject of rights, shows him to be still a pioneering thinker even in the 20th and 21st centuries, especially in view of the many failures over migration and asylum.'[17] The Jewish philosophers Emmanuel Lévinas and Jacques Derrida, in their philosophical arguments in the 20th century – against the background of the horror of the holocaust and the migrations from the Arab countries – went back to this idea of Kant's and set it in a new framework. They draw attention to the dilemma of hospitality, the tension between ethical demand – hospitality is an inalienable human right – and its political and legal enforcement. Following this line of thought, Jacques Derrida distinguishes between hospitality in the legal context and 'absolute hospitality',[18] which is present in the religious sources of Judaism and Christianity. Hospitality stands for the gratuitousness of a relationship, and goes beyond legal regulations governing social life. In the Rule of St Benedict hospitality is covered in Chapter 53: 'Let all guests who arrive be received as Christ, because He will say: "I was a stranger and you took Me in" (Mt 25:35).' Throughout history the guest house – the hospice – was always a place of protection, which took in the stranger without – initially – asking their name. It was a place of meeting free from ulterior motives. Guest and host, stranger and native, became a gift to each other in the experience of hospitality. The stranger is given the gift of hospitality, often enriched by a meal. The guest, the stranger to whom the door is opened, also expands the horizon to a new relationship of giving and taking, which creates space for something extra: 'A guest brings God in,' as Romano Guardini put it.[19] This connects with the absolute form of hospitality to which Derrida refers; it opens the relationship out to an 'economy of giving': 'The guest becomes the host's host... The master of the house is at home, but nonetheless he comes to enter his home through the guest – who comes from outside. The master thus enters from the inside, as if he came from the outside. He enters his home thanks to the visitor, by the grace of his guest (*par la grâce de son hôte*).'[20] Hospitality in its absolute form allows companionship to be experienced as 'gifted', as a mutual giving and receiving. This hospitality is deeply embedded in the Christ-event – through which the Church is constantly made new: the Eucharist is the sacrament of God's absolute hospitality, and the radical recognition of the other that here takes place as the deepest mystery of the faith becomes a sign for the recognition of others, without which companionship in peace and justice in the fast-moving spaces of the city is not possible. It allows the stranger over our threshold and allows us to find ourselves anew on each occasion through 'the grace of the guest': 'Do not neglect to show hospitality to strangers, for by doing that some have entertained angels without knowing it' (Heb 13.2). When we practise hospitality like this, we do not lose anything of our identity, but grow into the depths of the community of life with the God who is always greater.

It is therefore no small contribution to the 'future' of the city if the Church – and in a culture with a plurality of religions this can only be while recognising freedom of religion and in a new attitude of dialogue and ecumenical and inter-faith encounters – supports people in their 'arrival' in the city and helps them to develop a sense of belonging, without any disadvantage on social, cultural, religious or sexual grounds. If there come to be again first, second or third-class citizens, whether practically through difficulties in acquiring citizenship, or only 'invisibly', through cultural, religious or social exclusion, the city loses what makes it a city, the free and liberating community of the mass of citizens, men and women, the possibility offered of a good life on very different levels of community: family, economy, politics, society, culture and religion. Another part of this is creation of new ways of living faith, beyond the 'traditional' boundaries of the parish, which include ecumenical, inter-faith and inter-cultural projects. Part of this 'ecclesial conversion' is having the courage to try new forms of community, of participation at all levels of the Church, in dioceses, parishes, association, etc. The Church can only contribution to the 'freedom' of the city if it lives by the freedom of the gospel. Christians then take their direction from the gospel that Jesus of Nazareth preached: 'Repent, for the kingdom of God has come near' (Mk 1.15). It is on its way and meets new arrivals when there is 'salvation', in a good shared life in the city, when there is love, when reconciliation takes place, when hospitality is experienced and a hand is offered to the stranger, when those who were excluded and despised experience justice, and peace is made in the city.

Translated by Francis McDonagh

Notes

1. E.g. Benjamín Bravo/Alfons Vietmeier (ed.), *Gott wohnt in der Stadt. Dokumente des Internationalen Kongresses für Großstadtpastoral in Mexiko 2007*, Zürich and Berlin, 2008.

2. See 'Entrevista al Cardenal Jorge M. Bergoglio sj', in Virginia Azcuy (ed.), *Ciudad vivida. Prácticas de Espiritualidad en Buenos Aires*, Buenos Aires, 2014, pp 237-244.

3. See Margit Eckholt, 'Ernstzunehmende Anfragen. Die katholische Kirche und die Sekten in Lateinamerika', *Herder-Korrespondenz* 47 (1993), 250-255.

4. *Fifth General Conference of the Bishops of Latin America and the Caribbean, Aparecida, 13-31 May 2007, Concluding Document*, para 225: http://www.celam.org/aparecida/Ingles.pdf

5. On this see Margit Eckholt, 'Pfingstkirchen als Herausforderung für den Katholizismus', in: MD – *Materialdienst des Konfessionskundlichen Instituts Bensheim* 65 (2014), 56-59; 'Pfingstlich bewegt und befreiungstheologisch geerdet? Die "Pentekostalisierung" des Christentums in Lateinamerika und Herausforderungen für den lateinamerikanischen Katholizismus', in Polykarp Ulin Agan SVD (ed.), *Pentekostalismus – Pfingstkirchen. Akademie Völker und Kulturen* 2016/17, Siegburg, 2017, 33-57.

6. Interview of 28 July 2013, quoted from Jakob Egeris Thorsen, *Charismatic Practice and Catholic Parish Life. The Incipient Pentecostalization of the Church in Guatemala and Latin America*, Leiden and Boston, 2015, p. 220.

7. Margit Eckholt and Stefan Silber (ed.), *Glauben in Mega-Cities. Transformationsprozesse in lateinamerikanischen Großstädten und ihre Auswirkungen auf die Pastoral*, Ostfildern, 2014.

8. See Margit Eckholt, 'Citizenship, Sakramentalität der Kirche und empowerment. Eine dogmatisch-theologische und ekklesiologische Annäherung an den Begriff der "citizenship", in Virginia R. Azcuy and Margit Eckholt (ed.), *Citizenship – Biographien – Institutionen. Perspektiven lateinamerikanischer und deutscher Theologinnen auf Kirche und Gesellschaft*, Berlin and Zürich 2009, pp 11-40.

9. See Margit Eckholt (ed.), *Prophetie und Aggiornamento: Volk Gottes auf dem Weg. Eine internationale Festgabe für die Bischöfliche Aktion ADVENIAT*, Berlin, 2011.

10. See Stephan Günzel (ed.), *Raum. Ein interdisziplinäres Handbuch*, Stuttgart and Weimar, 2010; Nikolai Roskamm, *Dichte. Eine transdisziplinäre Dekonstruktion. Diskurse zu Stadt und Raum*, Bielefeld, 2011.

11. see, e.g., Frank Eckardt, *Soziologie der Stadt*, Bielefeld, 2004.

12. Judith Gruber, 'Kirche und Kultur. Eine spannungsvolle Identifizierung im Anschluss an *Gaudium et Spes*', Franz Gmainer-Pranzl and Magdalena Holztrattner (ed.), *Partnerin der Menschen – Zeugin der Hoffnung. Die Kirche im Licht der Pastoralkonstitution Gaudium et Spes*, Innsbruck and Vienna, 2010, pp 301-322, esp. p. 318.

13. The term comes from the book by Doug Saunders, *Arrival city: how the largest migration in history is reshaping our world* (London, 2010) and refers to the areas, often on the edges of cities, that tend to be occupied by newly arrived migrants.

14. Aristoteles, *Die Nikomachische Ethik. Aus dem Griechischen und mit einer Einführung und Erläuterungen versehen von Olof Gigon*, Munich, 7th ed., 2006, p. 285.

15. Immanuel Kant, 'Toward Perpetual Peace. A Philosophical Sketch', *Toward Perpetual Peace and Other Writings on Politics, Peace and History*, ed. Pauline Kleingeld, New Haven and London, 2006, p.82.

16. Immanuel Kant, 'Toward Perpetual Peace. A Philosophical Sketch', p. 82.

17. Rolf Gärtner, *Seid jederzeit gastfreundlich. Ein Leitbild für heutige Gemeindepastoral*, Ostfildern, 2012, 21-22.

18. Jacques Derrida, *Of Hospitality. Anne Dufourmantelle invites Jacques Derrida to respond*, Stanford, CA, 2000, pp 25-26.

19. Romano Guardini, *Briefe über Selbstbildung*. Bearbeitet von Ingeborg Klimmer, Mainz, 1978, 'Dritter Brief "Vom Geben und Nehmen, vom Heim und von der Gastfreundschaft"', pp 27-43, quotation from p. 37.

20. Derrida, *Of Hospitality*, p. 125 (translation adapted).

Transforming Our Cities:
Public Role of Faith and Theology

*Having engaged themselves for long with time and history, faith and
theology are invited today to reflect on space and geography. City space
presents ambiguity: On the one hand, it provides an ambience of freedom
and opportunity for cultivation of talents; on the other hand it is a haven
for the poor and the displaced. Neoliberal economy has turned the city
space into an arena of competition in which the poor are the losers,
as they experience many negations. Their cry is not heard, nor their
participation enlisted, even as city spaces are planned for them through
technocratic management. The problems of the poor, the migrants and
refugees are far from being solved basically due to persisting xenophobia
and for lack of deeper humanistic vision. Hence the challenge for theology
is to contribute with the help of other disciplines to an alternative vision
of life in the city space embodying the dreams and aspirations of the
poor and downtrodden and to foster dignified human existence and coexistence for all through solidarity, care and compassion. With our cities
turning increasingly multicultural, and pluri-religious, theology is further
challenged to come out with refreshing perspectives on pluralism and
coexistence in contemporary situation, moving beyond social contract
as the basis of societal constitution. Non-state actors and faith-inspired
voluntary groups could be catalysts with whom faith and theology could
interact to make common cause for the shaping of cities of the future as
humane communities and ecologically sound habitat. For theologians to
engage with such ideals for future cities would be a vocation to become
public intellectuals, seasoned by faith and echoing the Good News to the
Poor.*

I City and Its Opportunities

Many are the reasons and motives for people to move into the cities. For some, city is a place of wealth, comfort and high quality of living; for others, it offers facilities and opportunities for their skills and talents to flourish. No wonder, Aristotle characterized city as an indispensable place for 'living well' by which he meant a place for leading a life of happiness and for pursuing 'virtues' or talents.[1] In fact, unlike the hinterlands, cities with dense human proximity and concentration of talents create an ambience for the maximization of human capacities, for innovation, and create opportunities to practice justice and serve common good. Moreover, city is a place of freedom providing an atmosphere to cultivate individual self, free from social pressures, oppressive traditions and conventions.

Besides such ideals, in many developing countries, and increasingly also in the developed countries, city is the shelter to many victims of our world today – the impoverished, the landless, the abandoned, the displaced, the refugees, asylum-seekers, victims of ecological disasters, floating population from the countryside in search of labour and so on. City is some hope of survival in the midst of many deprivations the poor suffer. Chinese cities offer labour opportunities and draw people from hinterland, and Indian cities offer for many Dalits (the 'Untouchables' a sense of anonymity sparing them the humiliation of their oppressive caste-identity.

II The City Context of Theological Interventions

The social, economic and cultural opportunities cities offer is in stark contrast with the many darker sides they represent. Describing the cities in our global world, Zygmunt Bauman has this to say:

> Today, in a curious reversal of their historical role and in defiance of the original intentions of city builders and the expectations of city dwellers, our cities are turning swiftly from shelters against dangers into dangers' principal source. Dicken and Laustsen go as for as to suggest that the millennia-old link between civilization and barbarism is reversed. City life turns into a state of nature characterized by the rule of terror, accompanied by omnipresent fear.[2]

Moreover, modern technocratic city-planning seems to exacerbate especially the life of the poor, and, paradoxically, makes their life more insecure as never before, with constant danger of displacement of their dwellings, loss of occupations for their livelihood, and worst of all, negation of their human dignity – all in the name of city-development.

While the city as material space calls for the expertise of planners, architects, demographers, economists, and others, as a humanly constituted space it requires the support of *humanistic and social sciences*. Theology could join these disciplines to make its own contribution to this common project of a humane and eco-friendly cities of the future.[3]

But, modern theology has been preoccupied all along with temporal categories – the issues of time and history – in the study of scriptures, tradition and in hermeneutics. Since the *Sein und Zeit* of Heidegger, time and history have become important philosophical categories too. However, thanks to cultural and ecological studies, the category of *space* and geography have just begun to draw global attention. They have been long neglected. Faith-reflection needs to focus today on city as the space, the milieu of human coexistence in optimal environmental conditions. Increasingly the spaces of our cities are culturally, religiously, and ethnically plural and diversified. The arrangement of material space and planning of city may be a technical activity, but faith could contribute to create social spaces and ambience of mutuality and understanding among different ethnicities, religious and cultural groups. To be able to make its contribution, faith and theology need to take into account anthropological and social factors making up the city.

Negation of survival needs such as nutrition, housing, health care, clean environment, along with the experience of oppression, unemployment, and absence of educational opportunities are sources of insecurity and violence in cities across the world. Cities are where one experiences poverty in its old and new forms. The list is not complete if we do not include ethnic and racial and religious factors. One conveniently sidesteps these latter factors in analysis of the situation of cities. Further, in many cities of the world, religion far from being a solution is part of the problem. Religion and its symbols are used in conflict of power. For example, the Indian Muslims are increasingly marginalized and vulnerable minorities in Indian cities, and targets of violent attacks.[4] In many cities in the West there is, unfortunately, *institutionalized racism and religious prejudices* leading to expressions of violence. I think theologians and faith-communities in the West have the responsibility to challenge prophetically overt and covert expressions of racism and discrimination against minorities, ethnicities, migrants, and refugees at a time when these issues are threatening to break the European Union.

III Inter-Culturalism and Social Capital
On the one hand there is growing scepticism about the viability of multiculturalism. On the other hand, one would not like to go back to a policy of forced assimilation to the culture and tradition identified with the majority. It is at this juncture we realize the importance of *inter-culturalism*. Whereas multiculturalism advocates the right for diversity, interculturalism calls for openness to the other and communication with the other. This may not be achieved through psychological strategies or moral persuasion; these need to be accompanied by a different vision and appropriate policies and practices. A simple patronizing multiculturalism with acknowledgment of the legitimacy of plurality could lead to – as often feared – to ghettoization. This could be avoided through policies and practices of social, economic, and political equality and participation. To employ a classical distinction in sociology by Ferdinand Tönnies (later taken up by Max Weber), one of the important contributions faith and theology could make is to turn cities from *Gesellschaft* (society) into *Gemeinschaft* (community).

In modern times a model of future inter-cultural city was inspired by Sri Aurobindo of India and a French mystic Mirra Alfassa. Such a city called *Auroville* exists at the outskirts of Pondicherry, India. As an experiment, here people across nations, religions, races, languages live together and make up the city, foreshadowing the unity of humanity. It is set in the harmony of nature. Auroville embodies concretely the vision of alternative cities of the future. As the charter of this city states 'Auroville will be a place of unending education, of constant progress and a youth that never ages'.[5]

Robert Putnam made current the concept of *social capital*.[6] He makes a distinction between two aspects of social capital. One aspect of social capital is *bonding*, by which similar people bind themselves together in terms of common identity, shared values, history, tradition, religion etc. This has its own set of problems. It needs to be balanced by the other aspect of social capital, namely *bridging*, reaching out to the other. For the regeneration of urban life with the poor and disadvantaged as the focus, engaged faith-communities could help strengthen their social capital (both in bonding and bridging) and improve their quality of life in all respects. Social capital – especially with a balancing of bonding and bridging – can create the resilience necessary to overcome poverty in the city, which financial resources alone cannot do, and make up to some extent the appalling absence of sense of community.

IV Cry of the Poor in Cities

In the city of Pharaoh the cry of the poor was not heard. Our cities have their social and economic peripheries in innumerable slums with abysmal living conditions of many negations, where the voice of the poor and the victims are silenced. In Asia, Africa and Latin America, the poor live on the crumbs of the city created by forces of late global capitalism and neoliberal market. On the beautiful hills surrounding Rio de Janeiro are perched the *favelas* where more than a million live on the waste of the city. India has an urban population of 377 million – larger than the entire population of the USA! Of these, several millions live in slums like Dharavi in Mumbai, the largest slum in Asia. They sleep, cook, copulate and defecate in crammed spaces and pavements, with no security, no adequate nutrition, and healthcare. Slums are 'unintended cities'.[7] In Manila as many as 50% of the city population lives in slums. Till some years ago in the 'smoky mountain' of Tondo, Manila, thousands of families survived scavenging two million metric tons of city-waste. The poor in the slum also become victims of human trafficking, sexual abuse, dangerous medical experimentations, drug peddling and so on. One speaks of quality of life today. Where is the quality of life in our cities if we exclude people and deny a modicum of space for a dignified human life? With lack of open spaces and social isolation and no common spaces to meet and socialize – as the case in the villages – the poor opting to live in the city suffer immensely. There is an inextricable connection between poverty and environmental degradation. Poverty is the greatest pollutant, something one could experience palpably in the cities of the developing world.

Besides sound economy, infrastructure creation, environmental safety, recycling of waste, and governance, city requires a *human face* or as Emmanuel Levinas would put it, *'humanist urbanism'*.[8] Here faith and theology could contribute to create a human face to the city by addressing those issues and concerns of the people which economic, political, and cultural actors leave out of their purview. Faith perspectives and theology will take us beyond service delivering to the urban victims to their dignity as human beings. The Gospel option for the poor will translate into a city-planning that will start from bottom up, listening to the cry of the poor, attending to their conditions, responding to their needs and aspirations. For many, city pastoral work means how best we could bring faith to the people who are being secularized and save them from becoming materialists and consumerists. Today, we need to interpret faith and pastoral involvement in the light of *Gaudium et Spes*. Pastoral here refers to the nature of presence of the Church in the world. It means how Church, faith, and theology could address the larger issues of the city affecting the people across religion, geography, race, and culture.

As a theoretical premise to this faith-inspired enterprise we need to be aware that identity of city space, like other identities, are constructed relationally, and not in terms of an a priori essentialist conception. Spaces are ascribed meanings, and they become places, through interhuman encounters and relationality. What technocratic approach does is to take city space in its materiality leaving out the constructive aspect that makes space a humanly endowed reality which is an important presupposition for understanding the poor in the city spaces. That leads us to the next point.

V From Smart City to Compassionate City
Since 2008, smart city has become the stated objective of many states and business enterprises across the world.[9] This project proposes to transform cities and govern them through digital and other technological means of communication and automation by using available resources smartly. What dominates is the managerial approach to life in the city. It looks to me that the dominant city-projects of today are but contemporary application of the European Enlightenment paradigm of linear or dialectical human progress, development, and evolution. This paradigm has exercised such a great influence that even the Christian Scriptures were so interpreted as if God, like a city-planner and manager, had God's own map and *plan of salvation*!

All human problems cannot be solved by money; nor by technology and management. Enticing as it may sound, the project of smart city hides behind a multitude of human social, economic, and political issues. A humane city cannot be created and sustained without putting people above technology, which has only a service role to play. Policies and practices need to evolve after interaction and dialogue with the people and ascertaining their needs and aspirations. We succumb to the dangerous Enlightenment idea of progress and development when we place plans above dialogue. A process of dialogue will create cities from below. In short, the project of a city is a continuous process of dialogue and human interactions.

In situations of massive poverty and negation of basic needs of life and absence of adequate spaces in the city - as is the case especially in the so-called developing world - the project of smart city is likely to go to the advantage of the elite and the middle class, and may respond to the demands of the capital and market. What is forgotten is that there is a whole political process involved in the construction of the city where one has to come to terms with opposing classes and castes, different ethnicities, migrants, refugees, displaced people, and divergent economic interests. The problem with smart city is that it is a totally de-politicized project acting on presumed neutrality and impartiality vis-à-vis the inequality among the citizens, their contrasting socio-economic positions, and their conflicting interests.

As it is, city-planning is heavily influenced by the capital and the demands of the market with lip-service paid to the poor and those pushed to the margins of city-life. The city of the future, on the other hand, requires badly the spirit of human solidarity, radical care and infinite compassion which are really in shorty-supply today. We cannot expect these where human relationships are mediated by money and market. In fact, Friedrich Hayek was candid when he said love has no place in economics.[10] One of the most important contribution faith and theology could make for the future of our cities is to instil a new and alternative vision and orientation inspired by the spirit of love, care, and compassion. We are on a very weak foundation if we were to ground our contemporary social life and political institutions on the theory of an imaginary *social contract* (Jacques Rousseau) or to rely on justice to happen on a hypothetical *'original position'* (John Rawls). We are seeing the serious limits and weakness of such a basis which is at the bottom of the crisis of liberalism, capitalism, and market.[11] If we go by social contract and the logic of the market, there is no convincing answer for solidarity with the poor and the marginalized. The poor are to blame themselves for their lot, so goes the argument. Such being the situation, we are in need of alternative vision and perspectives that will illumine our common humanity, define our social life and interhuman relationships beyond the frame of self-interest and competition. This needs to get reflected in the way we construct and reconstruct cities with different priorities and values, other than the ones dictated by the market and consumerism.

Any amount of technology and managerial techniques cannot supplant human solidarity, care and compassion which will be the heart-beat of the cities of the future. Compassionate eyes see more and far than the most advanced technological means and projects. Like in the Gospel narrative, while the eyes of the elites are turned on the grandeur of the temple and its beauty, the compassionate eyes are turned to the poor widow. The quite offer of her mite in the temple invites praise from Jesus (Mk 12:41-44, Lk 21:1-4). The very people who contribute the lion's share in the creation of city through their hard labour – the poor, the migrants, the refugees, the discriminated – are ignored and sidelined, with no voice in shaping their habitat. Slums have become for planners an embarrassment. Instead of encountering them as human realities, one plans in order to eliminate them. This is diametrically opposed to the vision of a new Jerusalem Isaiah projected. ' I will rejoice in Jerusalem, and be glad in my people; no more shall be heard in it the sound of weeping and the cry of distress… They shall build houses and inhabit them. They shall not build and another inhabit ' (Is 65:19, 21-22).

The city is not simply a place, but a *milieu*. It is a milieu of community where peoples and groups can flourish by interconnecting and living in solidarity. Loving one's neighbour was relatively easy as long as the neighbour was of one's own colour, race, religion, culture and language. It has become a serious issue when we do not share any of these, and yet called to love and forge relationships. Neighbour is not simply a matter of physical proximity but a matter of negotiation and communication. The strangeness of the neighbour creates *xenophobia*. Now how does one move from the situation of xenophobia to *xenophilia* – that is the love for the stranger? How can we transform the growing mistrust that cuts off the vital human communication, by creating greater sense of confidence and solidarity among city-dwellers? Could faith and theology help people to make this transition?

It is significant that almost all the letters of Paul were written to city-dwellers, and addressing the problem of the communities there.[12] Using a rare expression, Paul enjoins the Philippians 'to live as good citizens (*politeuesthe*)' (Phil. 1:27). For Paul, city is a place of community, mutuality, relationships, completely different from today's image of city as a concentrated space of traders and consumers. He exhorts the citizens of Colossae to clothe themselves with compassion' (Col. 3:12) which should characterize their relationship in the community and in the larger society.

City as a community is a creation by all. Unsustainable city is the one where there is no community participation. Refusing to accept the participation of the poor, the migrants, and refugees will only add further to their vulnerability. In large cities, especially in developing countries, we note how the rich insulate themselves in the so called 'gated-communities' by erecting walls and fences and barring access to the poor. The wealthy also ensure for themselves the best lands and greeneries, privatizing public spaces. If the Church wants to be a witnessing Church in such situations, one of the best ways is to make available Church buildings, premises, infrastructure and facilities for the common purposes of the citizens, especially the vulnerable ones. This means to be a Church without walls. In this way, the Church will be entering into genuine communication with the local community, and the people will begin to feel that the Church is there for them. These are the ways to create solidarity and community. All this will help also to allay the fears and suspicion by 'secularists' and by peoples of other religious traditions about the motive of the Church in its city-involvement.

VI City and Ecology

The present model of development takes place at the cost of nature. Unbridled global consumerism continues to create mountains of waste (two billion tonnes in 2016) in our cities, posing serious threat also for the health and survival of the humans. Pope Francis, tells us that the planning of the city should be such that it chimes not only with canons of aesthetics, but most importantly that it contributes to *the quality of life* and facilitates human interconnectedness, solidarity and sense of belonging. The pope dreams of another model of city. To quote his words,

> How beautiful those cities which overcome paralysing mistrust, integrate those who are different and make this very integration a new factor of development! How attractive are those cities which, even in their architectural design, are full of spaces which connect, relate and favour the recognition of others![13]

Pope Francis in his *Laudato Si'* invites planners to consider the environmental impact of city projects and integrate the human and the social with the natural environment.

Alternative vision concerns also development of an environmentally sustainable landscapes and way of life in the cities. The environmental decline and climate change caused by city for its residents and for the world may not be responded only by technocratic solutions or change in urban planning. It calls for a new mindset and a way of life that is respectful of nature and responsible in the use of its resources, something to which faith and theology could richly contribute.

VII Faith-Inspired and Humanistic Non-State Actors

Voluntary groups and non-state actors (NGOs) have their hands on the pulse of the people and their feet on the rough ground at the bottom. Civil society and social movements– which autocratic states tend to suppress – have a great role to play in shaping our cities echoing the hope and aspirations of the people, especially the marginalized and the discriminated ones. An encounter of faith and theology with civil society initiatives and social movements could become mutually beneficial and strengthen the common cause of creating peoples' cities.

A significant document of the Anglican Church titled *Faithful Cities* reminds us what faith-sources could represent vis-à-vis the cities of today. It notes,

> Despite its ambivalent history, and its capacity to incite hatred and conflict, religious faith is still one of the richest, most enduring and most dynamic sources of energy and hope for cities. Faith is a vital— and often essential— resource in the building of relationships and communities. In the values they promote, in the service they inspire, and in the resources they command, faith-based organizations make a decisive contribution to their communities.'[14]

These grassroots organizations may not place much value on traditional religious establishments, but they represent, so to say, *liquid religion*. Their fluidity is a great advantage for effective, timely and relevant interventions in urban social and political processes. Dialogue and cooperation among faith-inspired organizations and humanistically-oriented non-state actors could reinforce the work of each other for transforming our cities. Faith and theological reflections could accompany the non-state actors. They can jointly play a prophetic role of protest and resistance to a model of the city that is structurally anti-poor and inspirationally pro-greed. Such a city is diametrically opposed to the values and vision the Gospel and its Good News to the poor stands for.

VIII Challenge to Theology

The dominant theology has been grappling with the question of how to reconcile faith with modernity. But today theological question needs to shift and address the question of poverty and material deprivation, justice, issues of human dignity, human rights, community and social cohesion, drawing from the rich sources of faith for action and active engagement. This has implications for theological method and orientation. To be able to respond to the life of the city, for example, theology needs to increasingly take on narrative form embedded in life-experience of the people. For lack of this kind of approach, the institutions pursuing theology today, unfortunately, have very little public influence. The challenges our cities offer is an opportunity for theology to break loose of its self-isolation and enter into conversation with wider issues and questions taken up by non-state actors (NGOs) today, so vital for coexistence and harmony.

Further, theology could widen its scope and contribute to create *public intellectuals* who would advocate the cause of an equitable and environmentally sustainable cities. Public advocacy of the issues touching the life of the city – especially its poor – and formulation of economic and environmental policies to redress the persisting woes and enhance the quality of life for all – these are what engaged faith, Church, and theology could do hand in hand with non-state actors.

Out of these experiences we need to think of new areas of study and research on the part of theologians as public intellectuals with the future of the city as the focus. Though cities across the world share many things in common, yet, undeniably there are remarkable differences deriving from past history, the social, political condition in each case. Theologians could look into some of the most pressing issues and concerns and identify areas of reflection, study and research in context. This would support the formulation of urban public policies bearing upon the promotion of social justice and cohesion, and protection of the environment. This can be done meaningfully when theology and theological researches are shaped by other disciplines, and theology itself takes on the character of public theology.

IX Conclusion

In former times, walls with watch-towers erected around the city served to protect the citizens. Far from havens of security, today our cities have become centres of terror and insecurity. Correctly understood human rights are the real new security of our future cities.[15] However, human rights are not the privilege of some; it is applicable to all. It is not that we lack human rights; the real problem is *the hypocrisy* in the selective application of human rights, to the advantage of the already rich and powerful. Hence, I think today it is important to focus on the rights of the poor, which includes the right to city.

Cities are also spaces filled with *community obligations* the fulfilling of which expresses a sense of solidarity and interdependence. Promoting the participation and cooperation of all in building the city could help overcome the opposition between residents and strangers. Faith and theology are called upon to assist in the process of making everyone in the city feel at home, what the German language expresses as *Beheimatung*. The language of 'hospitality' often employed today appears to me as an ambiguous concept. It does not express the much needed *sense of belonging*. Here is the crux of the question.

Care and compassion for the poor and the marginalized, upholding justice and rights of the victims, facilitation of their active participation in the life of the city, the quality of social relationships, harmony and cohesion among the diverse groups of the people in the city – these should become new parameters and criteria for evaluating the cities of the future. This humanistic criteria will override the assessment of cities on the basis of their physical structure and technocratic management.

Further, it is important to remember that human societies are not perfect blueprints nor cute photo finish. There is a *price to be paid* for the richness and diversity our cities represent. I mean we need to be prepared for a certain amount of *uncertainty, unpredictability, disruption and disorganization*. Theology and faith will need to step in when one would like to give up the value of pluralism for the sake of an imagined perfect order of the society. Faith and theology could play a public role by focusing on i*nterculturalism, communication, dialogue and negotiation* reaching out to the culturally, religiously, ethnically, and linguistically different other.

Notes

1. Aristotle, *Politics* (London: Penguin Books, 1992), 1252b27.
2. Zygmunt Bauman, *Does Ethics Have a Chance* (Cambridge MA: Harvard University Press, 2008), p. 65.
3. Space does not permit me to go into a discussion on the legitimacy and manner of faith-intervention and theological contribution in socio-political issues, especially in post-secular societies. I have treated this elsewhere. See, Felix Wilfred, T*heology for an Inclusive World* (Delhi: ISPCK, 2019); *Theology to Go Public* (Delhi: ISPCK, 2013); see also Nigel Biggar – Linda Hogan (eds), *Religious Voices in Public Places* (Oxford: Oxford University Press, 2009).
4. Cf. Laurent Gayer and Chrisophe Jaffrelot, eds., *Muslims in Indian Cities* (Noida: HarperCollins, 2012).
5. https://www.auroville.org/contents/1 [accessed on 30 September, 2018]; see also Anu Majumdar, Auroville, *A City for the Future* (Noida: HarperCollins, 2017).
6. See Robert Putnam, *Bowling Alone. The Collapse and Revival of American Community* (New York: Simon & Schuster Paperback, 2000).
7. Cf. Jai Sen, 'The Unintended City', in *The Oxford Anthology of the Modern Indian City. Making and Unmaking the City,* edited by Vinay Lal (Delhi: Oxford University Press, 2013) pp. 145-154.
8. Cf. Michael L. Morgen, *Levinas's Ethical Politics* (Bloomington: Indiana University Press, 2016), p. 179.
9. In June 2015, the Government of India launched 'Smart Cities Mission' with the aim of developing one hundred cities, technologically oriented and sustainable.
10. Cf. Friedrich A. von Hayek, *The Constitution of Liberty* (Chicago: Chicago University Press, 1960).
11. See *The Economist* September 15 – 21, 2018, dealing with the crisis of liberalism.
12. Cf. Steve Walton et al. eds, *The Urban World and the First Christians* (Grand Rapids: William B. Eerdmans, 2017).
13. *Evangelii Gaudium* no. 210.
14. The quotation is from *Faithful Cities* – a document of the Anglican Church, as quoted in *International Journal of Public Theology* 2008/1 p. 17. This document from the Anglican Church was preceded by Faith in the City (1985), different in tone, approach, and orientation.
15. See the special issue 'Human Security', *Concilium* 2018/2.

Part Three: Ethical Reflections on Urbanisation and its Challenges

Cities and their Global Responsibility: Reflections on Social Ethics from a German Perspective

MICHELLE BECKA

Cities and conurbations in Europe, and especially in Germany face various social and ecological challenges. But while local social problems are usually immediately visible through phenomena such as gentrification or social segregation, ecological problems linked to the use of resources and CO2 emissions tend to be less visible here than in other parts of the world. This article calls for social and ecological issues not to be separated, and focuses on the interweaving of local and global responsibility. Cities play a particular role in the recognition of this dual responsibility, as is demonstrated by issues of climate justice, social integration and city networking.

Mumbai, Rio, Cape Town – none of the mega-cities is located in Germany or Europe. Fast-growing informal settlements, a very high population density alongside inadequate infrastructure – these are rarities in this part of Europe. Instead, Germany – more than other European countries – is characterised by having a large number of medium-sized cities and small towns. And yet there are social and ecological challenges in Europe's cities, especially Germany's, which this article will attempt to outline and consider from a perspective of social ethics. Central to this reflection is the interweaving of the local and global responsibility of cities, exemplified by questions of climate justice, social integration and transnational solidarity.

A central social problem is that of high property prices and rents, which have led to a dramatic shortage of affordable housing in German cities. This is no longer true just of the large cities themselves, but also of the

61

so-called metropolitan regions: families and people on low wages struggle to find adequate housing. This development is taking place alongside gentrification: tenants are being driven out by the rising costs. This leads to an increase in segregation, which becomes the spatial illustration of social inequality. Social intermingling, and the mixing of generations and nationalities, is happening less. This especially true of large cities, where social segregation is more marked than ethnic segregation.[1] When the two types of segregation are superimposed, however, they are mutually reinforcing: there is a correlation between ethnic and spatial concentration, poverty and unemployment.[2] Increasing socio-spatial inequality reappears in the schools and is thus further reinforced, making integration difficult. Prospects for training and jobs in such areas are meagre. There are numerous inadequacies in policies for promoting integration, ranging from inadequate basic provisions (a lack of housing and language courses) to everyday racism, which remains a problem.

Among ecological problems the main complaint is of high air pollution in some cities, especially through goods vehicles fuelled by diesel. Much less attention is given, however, to other, less obvious environmental and climate problems. This is because since the 1980s various environmental policies have been introduced that have improved the quality of life in many cities. Nevertheless these achievements disguise more recent deficits, especially in dealing with climate change, which is our most urgent current problem, though less evident in cities of the global North because the results of the excessive use of resources and high CO2 emissions are mainly felt in other parts of the world.[3] This illustrates the interlocking of the local and global aspects of climate, to which we shall have to return.

I Sustainability – local and global

One of the factors making sustainable (urban) development more difficult is that social and environmental issues are too often considered separately or even as in opposition. For example, in Germany the energy-saving regulation introduced in 2007 requires improving the insulation of old buildings. For renters, however, these generally sensible measures are the prelude to often massive rent increases. Those who cannot afford the high rents have to get out. A measure causing social problems can be justified by appeal to mitigating climate change, and the supply of affordable housing is reduced. The principle of sustainability, which is relevant to social ethics and politics, says that no more resources should be consumed than can regrow, regenerate or be replaced over time: it introduces a time parameter into the concept of responsible behaviour. Part of the obligation is to take account simultaneously of both environmental and social (and economic) considerations. Pope Francis too, in *Laudato Si'* (49) emphasises that: 'Today, however, we have to realize that a true ecological approach always becomes a social approach; it must integrate questions of justice in debates on the environment, so as to hear *both the cry of the earth and the cry of the poor* (italics in original).' This does not happen enough in practice. One reason is that in a highly complex society areas of work are divided, with the result that responsibility for the environment and responsibility for social justice are distinct areas. In view of the great complexity of political connections this is completely necessary and sensible, but if the distinction of responsibilities becomes a division and there is no overall sense of direction, there are blind spots and contradictory measures. Christian social ethics – and not just since *Laudato Si'* – expands human responsibility for our actions beyond the interpersonal and institutional into the non-human environment. But it remains a single responsibility: we have to counter artificial divisions that try to set ecological issues in opposition to social issues. This eco-social responsibility has not only local but also transnational dimensions. According to Article 3.1 of the 1992 Climate Framework Convention, 'The Parties should protect the climate system for the benefit of present and future generations of humankind, on the basis of equity and in accordance with their common but differentiated responsibilities and respective capabilities. Accordingly, the developed country Parties should take the lead in combating climate change and the adverse effects thereof.'[4] The industrialised countries have contributed to climate change over a long period and are today, because of their resources, better able to transform their life-styles in a way that protects the climate. Consequently, by virtue of the 'Polluter pays' principle, and because obligation presupposes ability, they have a greater responsibility to contribute to slowing climate change. Germany and the EU as a whole are not facing up to this responsibility; the measures are not sufficient. Germany, once a pioneer in environmental and climate matters, is also not meeting its own goals: the 2017 Climate Protection Report makes it clear that the original goal of reducing greenhouse gas emissions by 40% (from 1999 values) by 2020 cannot be met. The expected reduction is currently 32%.[5] Another factor is that awareness in the population of our worldwide responsibility because we are all affected

63

by climate change is low, and we need a powerful lobby for a policy to protect the climate.

Laudato Si' demands responsibility from the richer countries and calls our lifestyle into question; it insists that it is not enough to maintain our existing growth and consumption model and simply add a few compensatory mechanisms. Francis talks about rethinking and repentance – and this reorientation needs to be understood both individually and structurally (though Francis underplays the structural dimension). Limited resources mean that the Western lifestyle cannot be universalised, but on grounds of justice the countries of the global South cannot simply be barred from consumption and 'development'. Logically this implies a need to change consumption patterns and lifestyles in the more industrialised countries, but this is not explained in political and public debate. It is hardly ever stated in public that a more modest lifestyle would be necessary in the countries of the global North to make possible a good life for all.[6] It is understandable that people should be concerned with maintaining or improving their status quo, and so talk of restrictions is unpopular, and parties will hardly win votes with this platform. But it is not right to exclude moral responsibility from the debate on grounds of convenience. In the sphere of moral education there is work to be done to explain the consequences of our lifestyle and, even more forcefully, a need to insist on policies that take climate and environmental problems seriously if we are to create structures that promote climate-friendly behaviour (through taxation, subsidies, infrastructure, etc.). The scientific recommendations and strategies have been available for a long time; for example, the cities paper of the German government's Advisory Council on Global Change (WBGU) spells out a convincing set of guidelines and offers practical suggestions. In recognition of our common but distinct responsibilities, we need a determined implementation of the core recommendations in the cities of the global North, especially in Germany.[7] The This obligation applies also to the Church, as a part of civil society. Many Church institutions, such as conference centres, are trying to reduce CO2 emissions and implement other measures to prevent climate change and protect the environment. Nevertheless, action on climate change needs to be 'louder' and clearer if *Laudato Si'* is to be more than a theoretical essay.

Questions of sustainability are closely connected with those of justice. One place in which they arise in cities is in connection with town planning. According to the German Advisory Council on Climate

Change, 'In investment decisions and architectural competitions in cities priority should be given to the poorest 40% rather than the richest 5% of the population.'[8] This apparently simple rule makes sense in terms of justice, as it would help to resist segregation. This can be interpreted as an expression of the option for the poor and equally as an application of John Rawls' second principle of justice, which states that economic and social inequality should bring the greatest possible benefit to the least advantaged. The least advantaged should therefore be at the centre of urban investment decisions. If in addition these decisions are taken not for the poorest 40% but – in accord with the principle of subsidiarity, which implies participation – with them, this raises the question how this is to happen. Equal conditions – for example, when everyone has a vote or when public discussions are organised – are not enough to ensure justice in participation, because the situations of those involved are too unequal. There is a need for appropriate processes, practical empowerment strategies or long-term community building strategies that enable disadvantaged population groups to take part and accompany the processes in an appropriate way, without a relapse into paternalism.

II City networks as particular actors
The interlocking of local and transnational levels of behaviour is illustrated by the growing importance of city networking. Cities are not only affected in a particular way by the challenges we have outlined and by international developments, but are also increasingly proving to be a significant actor in global connections. Their goals are often concerned with spatial development, which are easier to achieve in an association than separately, but in addition they also pursue political goals (policies on the climate, peace and migration), and so assume responsibility for tasks traditionally performed by the state. Transnational city networks are introducing a new level into political activity. Their activity is often fed by dissatisfaction with national politics. 'The increased assumption of responsibility by cities and associations of cities for the process of transforming urban areas creates a poly-centric structure of responsibility in which responsibilities are not exclusively ranked hierarchically, but distributed horizontally over several levels of the governance system.'[9] The transformative potential of cities is being recognised and exploited globally. The report of the Advisory Council on Climate Change talks about 'transformative urban

governance'.[10] What this means can be illustrated by city alliances on climate issues and immigration.

The biggest transnational city network is the Climate Alliance. 'Climate Alliance was founded in 1990 when a group of 33 institutions comprised of 12 municipalities from Germany, Austria and Switzerland as well as 6 indigenous organisations of the Amazon Basin met in Frankfurt, Germany, motivated take action against the climatic changes taking place.'[11] The Alliance claims a membership of 1700 local authorities, motivated by the recognition that global climate issues must be tackled locally. To this end they have set themselves the obligation to reduce CO2 emissions by 10% every five years, which is a more ambitious goal than that set by national governments.[12] To encourage cooperation on issues of migration and integration, in 2008 the CLIP network (Cities for Local Integration Policy) was founded. 'The economic and cultural integration of migrants represents both a challenge and an opportunity for all Member States. Many of the challenges are dealt with at the local level. Cities and local authorities have a vital role to play, not only in the implementation of integration policies, but also in the development of innovative policies on housing, education and cultural diversity.'[13] In view of this the cities that make up the network exchange ideas and seek to learn from each other's experience, to share examples of best practice, and engage in research to improve their policies to increase their effectiveness.

City networks are an expression of global solidarity for the purpose of strengthening local actors. There is a link between them because cities around the world are alike in many ways: they are areas of plurality and urbanity, in the sense of civilised living, they have specific environments but similar problems and sometimes struggle with their dependence on national authorities. This recognition of the similarity of cities across borders creates a degree of connection that bridges the categories of North and South. This link enables them to defend their common interests and each other; it is a form of international solidarity. It is an important step in the understanding of global solidarity, as not so much a single solidarity, but plural or rather a worldwide network of solidarities, to which the city networks can make a contribution. Nevertheless, as in other solidarity relationships there is a need to guard against exclusivity: it would be regrettable if the strengthening of the links between cities led to a (greater) weakening of their links with their rural hinterlands and produced competition. On balance, however, transnational networks make sense. They strengthen cities over against national bodies and thereby promote increased competence, practical governance structures and new forms of subsidiarity. At local level citizens gain opportunities for strengthening their identity and developing plans, and social cohesion is increased; networking to some extent makes local ties global. The growth of participation and representation is also significant for democracy. And since cities can be more flexible in their action than nation states, they can be pioneers in responding to challenges as they arise, as shown by the examples mentioned above.

III Sharing the city

Regional and national networks take on a similar function within a country. In summer 2018 a particular city initiative in Germany reacted to the ending of the rescue programmes in the Mediterranean that left migrants dying. At first three cities, Düsseldorf, Cologne and Bonn, formed an alliance and wrote to Chancellor Merkel as follows: 'We agree with you that there must be a European solution for the acceptance, the asylum process and the integration or repatriation of refugees. Until a European solution is agreed with all those involved, we must as a matter of urgency resume rescue efforts in the Mediterranean and ensure that the people who are rescued are taken in. Our cities are able and willing to take in refugees who are in difficulty – just as other cities and communities in Germany have already offered to do.'[14] This alliance is a strong protest against the criminalisation of refugees and tries to save human life. It combines criticism of higher political levels with action and commitment at local level, and also provides an alternative to the indifference that characterises public debate. At the same time the initiative points to the fact that those best placed to deal with integration are people at local level. Equity argues for national schemes and criteria for the reception of refugees by communities, and it would be wrong to challenge the basic competence of national authorities. Nonetheless local possibilities and the experience of local actors demand a degree of flexibility. Specifically, this can, as in the case of the three-city initiative, turn into a request to take in more people because certain cities are in a position to do so. Ultimately it means paying attention to local characteristics, needs and expertise and valuing it – and supporting it with the necessary funding.

IV Integration

This brings us back to the question of how people of different nationalities, cultures and religions live alongside each other, some with a migration background and others without. It is in the cities that we discover whether community and integration succeed.[15] Integration always implies reciprocity. This includes willingness to integrate on the one hand alongside acceptance on the other. A group that is willing to integrate can only integrate if there is a minimum of interest on the part of the host society.[16]

Because the main factors in successful integration are collaboration and participation, it is precisely these that must be made possible: immigrants must be able to take part in community life. The German Expert Council on Migration and Integration identifies different interlocking dimensions of participation: According to this definition, integration is about striving to achieve 'equal participation to the furthest extent possible in the key areas of social life'. This places the economic (employment, income, training, etc.), the cultural (language, education, religion, traditions, etc.), the social (community, living, circle of friends, identification, etc.) and the political (civil participation, parties, associations, etc.) aspects of life at the centre of the analysis.'[17]

Ensuring participation does not replace individual initiative in these various fields, but does draw attention to the forms of support required to make individual initiative possible. For example, willingness to learn the language must be matched by the provision of language courses (and making it possible for people to take part), etc. Structural support, the creation of basic conditions by local authorities, must be supplemented by other, 'softer' factors. A basic condition for enabling people to live side by side is avoiding polarisation in attitudes, opposing a supposedly clear 'we' to 'the others'. This not only makes it more difficult for people to integrate as they arrive, but also creates a problem for cohesion between different sections of the community. Even if society, as opposed to community, does not require friendly relations, respect for one another is nevertheless necessary if we are to form a society despite our diversity: basic sense of common identity is required. Integration in society means tolerating, respecting and, at best, appreciating difference – and at the same time looking for and nurturing a basis for cohesion.

Among the many factors that play a role in this process, a brief reference is appropriate here to religion and faith communities, which is thoroughly ambivalent. 'If the primary function of religions is to codify the difference between members and non-members of a community, they would tend to be an obstacle to social integration.'[18] At the same time, however, religions can be seen as stores of social capital. Social capital makes it possible to form ties to others within a group, which strengthens the group. As Lesch emphasises, welcoming strangers into this group of people with the same language or religion creates a feeling of security and acceptance, but this experience of security within the group then provides a basis for making contacts outside this group.[19] The creation of relationships of trust reduces insecurities and so contributes to confidence in activity in the new social context. Strengthening this bridging function of social capital turns out to be the central task of Church communities, and interdenominational and interfaith initiatives active in cities. This can take place through language communities such as exist in some German dioceses. Of course a strict separation between language communities and territorial communities is not desirable, since a feature of catholicity is that it crosses national and linguistic boundaries. But language communities can be important for social capital because they make Catholics with a migration background feel at home and give them a sense of identity – and in this way enable them to network beyond this small community. It is also important for these communities to be able to feel part of the city community or territorial community. Brigitta Sassin not only uses the example of Frankfurt's City Church to illustrate the diversity it contains (23 languages spoken), but also cites an example of best practice in the shape of the German-speaking parish in the Gallus area, which values the languages and countries of origin of parishioners and links this with a comprehensive support outreach.[20] The parish's outreach work has given rise to networks and initiatives supported by a variety of people, which have contributed to community building in the area. In addition, there is also collaboration with the local mosques – in this case the Church's role not exclusive, but inclusive.

Strengthening participation and cohesion and avoiding polarisation: this has been shown in these examples to be the key to facing the challenges cities face, both within the cities and internationally: between ecology and social issues, between those who have only recently come to live in the city and those who have lived in the city for some time.

These are not sufficient, but necessary, conditions for a just city, one which allows all to enjoy a good life, but a good life that does not make a good life for others (across the world) impossible.

Translated by Francis McDonagh

Notes

1. Cf J. Goebel und L. Hoppe, *Das sozio-ökonomische Panel, Ausmaß und Trends sozialräumlicher Segregation in Deutschland, Abschlussbericht einer Studie im Auftrag des Bundeministeriums für Arbeit und Soziales*, Berlin: 2015, p. 8: https://www.bmas.de/SharedDocs/Downloads/DE/PDF-Publikationen/a-305-7-abschlussbericht-ausmass-trends-sozialraeumlicher-segregation.pdf;jsessionid=4683D0A53758031BFEF390074F85A6B7?__blob=publicationFile&v=1 , accessed 15.08.2018.
2. For example, Frankfurt am Main is a city with a very international character, containing very different groups of immigrants and displaying wide income disparities. Cf A. Treichler, 'Die Wahrnehmung, Interpretation und Bearbeitung sozialer Ungleichheit in und durch die Global City Frankfurt am Main', in P. Pielage et al. (ed.), *WISO-Diskurs, Soziale Ungleichheit in der Einwanderungsgesellschaft. Kategorien, Konzepte, Einflussfaktoren*, Berlin, 2012: https://www.bibb.de/dokumente/pdf/Soziale_Ungleichheit_in_der_Einwanderungsgesellschaft_FES.pdf (accessed 4/01/2019), pp 154-171. It is impossible to explore here the extremely complex interrelations between economic, social and cultural factors that go to produce the spatial signs of inequality.
3. In addition, (big) cities generally have more climate protection measures than small cities and communities. The reason for this is denser housing and poor infrastructure (such as a lack of local public transport outside big cities) and especially life style and habits (SUVs, the lack of ecological construction, etc.).
4. *United Nations Framework Convention on Climate Change*: https://unfccc.int/resource/docs/convkp/conveng.pdf, accessed 02.01.2019.
5. Cf Bundesministerium für Umwelt, Naturschutz und nukleare Sicherheit, *Klimaschutzbericht* 2017, Berlin, 2018, pp 7-8.
6. The Bolivian idea of 'living well' calls for a good life for all people instead of a better life for a few. Putting this into practice may raise many questions, but it offers stimulating suggestions.
7. Cf Wissenschaftlicher Beirat der Bundesregierung Globale Umwelveränderungen (WBGU), *Der Umzug der Menschheit: Die Transformative Kraft der Städte*, Berlin, 2016, pp 28-29; For the English version, German Advisory Council on Global Change (WBGU), *Humanity on the move: Unlocking the transformative power of cities*, Berlin, 2016: https://www.wbgu.de/en/flagship-reports/fr-2016-urbanization/, accessed 07.01.2019.
8. WBGU, *Der Umzug der Menschheit: Die Transformative Kraft der Städte*, p. 29.
9. WBGU, *Der Umzug der Menschheit*, p. 24.
10. WGBU, *Der Umzug der Menschheit*.
11. Climate Alliance, 'The Growth of a Movement', http://www.climatealliance.org/about-us.html, accessed 07.01.2019.
12. Climate Alliance, 'Tangible Targets': http://www.climatealliance.org/about-us.html.
13. Cities for Local Integration Policy, 'About CLIP': https://www.eurofound.europa.eu/about-clip, accessed 07.01.2019.
14. See the statement from the Düsseldorf city authorities on the internet: https://www.duesseldorf.de/aktuelles/news/detailansicht/newsdetail/duesseldorf-koeln-und-bonn-angebot-und-appell-zur-fluechtlingshilfe-an-kanzlerin-merkel-1.html, accessed 07.01.2019.
15. The next two paragraphs draw on M. Becka, 'Integration der Migranten – Integration der

Gesellschaft', in M. Heimbach-Steins (ed.), *Zerreißprobe Flüchtlingsintegration, Freiburg im Breisgau*, 2017.

16. Discussions about multiculturalism have for some time made the point that all involved have to display a degree of openness and even a tolerance of uncertainty. This is also relevant to questions of integration. And yet it is here that there is a particular difficulty, because fears often dominate or prevent encounters. This is currently one of the main challenges.

17. Sachverständigenrat Deutscher Stiftungen für Migration und Integration, *Deutschlands Wandel zum modernen Einwanderungsland. Jahresgutachten 2014*, Berlin 2014, p. 20. English version: https://www.svr-migration.de/wp-content/uploads/2014/11/SVR-annual-report-2014_nine-core-messages.pdf.

18. W. Lesch, 'Religion als Ressource in Einwanderungsgesellschaften?', in J. Könemann and M.-T. Wacker (ed.), *Flucht und Religion. Hintergründe – Analysen – Perspektiven*, Münster, 2018, pp 211-228, quotation from p. 219.

19. W. Lesch, 'Religion als Ressource in Einwanderungsgesellschaften?', op. cit.

20. See B. Sassin, 'Migranten – Rückgrat der Pastoral von morgen', in P. Hundertmark and H. Schöne-mann (ed.), *Pastoral hinter dem Horizont. Eine ökumenische Denkwerkstatt*, Katholische Arbeitsstelle für missionarische Pastoral, *KAMP kompakt*, vol. 6, Speyer, pp 182-189.

Faith and Religion in Globalized Megacities: A View from Manila

DANIEL FRANKLIN PILARIO

Against secularization theory and its variants, religions abound in cities not only in our globalized postmodern times but as they have always been. The fluid networks of cultures provide a fertile backdrop for their proliferation and flourishing. Two observations about religion in the megacity Manila: first, the everyday religious practice of grassroots communities, mostly dubbed by outsiders as popular religiosity, to our assessment is the natural expression of all religions in contact with others. Second, the institutional Church becomes an ambivalent force in this context: on the one hand, it provides an alternative system to what the oppressive political and global economic structures neglect; on the other hand, it still needs to open itself more to contending and plural social forces characteristic of urban cosmopolitan cultures.

Have the gods left the city? Or have they come back with a vengeance? Where can we find them now? Popular imagination has ambivalent notions of the divine presence in urban and cosmopolitan contexts. On the one hand, we have metaphorical 'sin cities' deserving of God's wrath and punishment. On the other hand, all religions vigorously flourished in the world's main cities. Where shall we locate religion in our present globalized cities? Does it serve the well-being of peoples it was meant to? I intend to answer these questions from the perspective of Manila, one of the world's megacities. This reflection is divided into three parts: the discourse of religion in modernity; contours of the faith life among grassroots communities in the city; the assessment of institutional Church as public religion.

I The Adventures of Religion in the City

Secularization theory has a view of religion that fades at the onset of modern rationality. As modernity advances, it argues, religion retreats from the social milieu. In the words of C. Wright Mills, religion will 'disappear altogether except, possibly, in the private realms.'[1] The modern 'iron cage of reason' is supposed to drive away the religious relegating it to one sphere of life – the private – rather than as one all-pervading narrative. Max Weber calls the 'disenchantment of the world' parallel to contemporary sociologists like Peter Berger's withdrawal of the 'sacred canopy' where 'all of social life receives ultimate meaning binding on everybody.'[2] Thus, the local and the rural overflow with religion while the cosmopolitan and the urban are bereft of it. Though Berger recants this secularist tune at a later time,[3] its remnants still persist in the 'spiritual but not religious' (SBNR) or 'believing but not belonging' discourses in contemporary sociological analyses.[4] What disappears is public religion, but not private spirituality. People still believe but do not want to belong to traditional institutions.

The secularist narrative of religion can be read hand in hand with its evolutionary cousins.[5] Robert Bellah's *Religion and Human Evolution*[6] theorizes that religions evolve from the tribal, to the archaic and to the axial ages; from ritual to mythical to theoretical. The evolutionary logic is not a new narrative: Karl Jaspers already periodized history into four stages, e.g., Promethean, ancient, axial and modern histories; while August Comte divided sociology into three progressive states, i.e., theological, metaphysical and scientific. This is the point I want to establish: If we push the evolutionary logic to its limits, religions will soon disappear, or hide in some private realms of social consciousness as it is supplanted by the scientific technological paradigm in the present cosmopolitan and global city.

But there is another competing narrative worth recounting. Religions and cities in fact have never been strangers to one another. Religions created cities around them; and urban locations become a fertile network for the flourishing of religious beliefs. In the first millennium BCE, for instance, Buddhist and Jain monasteries started in the outskirts of cities like Taxila or Varanasi in India; and as the temples became popular, great cities thrived around them. In other instances, urban mobility takes over older religious sites and transform them into cities like Delhi, which was once the location of ancient Sufi shrines, or Punjab, which was built over a famous centre of Sikh religion.[7] The first cities that emerged in Mesopotamia around 3200 BCE were also organized around temples. Religion provided cohesion and control among the population, thus, explaining the intricate relationship between the notion of 'god' and 'king' in the city as the centre of power.[8] Though the Christian movement started in small villages around Palestine, its spread was facilitated by the system of urban centres across the Roman Empire – Jerusalem, Antioch, Corinth, Alexandria, Ephesus, Damascus, Edessa, Carthage and others. The historian Rodney Stark writes: 'Of the twenty-two largest cities in the empire, four probably still lacked a Christian church by the year 200.'[9] The intersection of cultures in these cities made possible the spread of Christianity to the urban areas of China or India in the first millennium of the Christian era. In short, the city and cosmopolitan urban centres are not inimical to religions as the secularization theories want us to believe. Religion has thrived on these centres' landscapes, transforming them according to its worldview, while at the same time being transformed by their divergent practices of politics and commerce.

If these examples are too ancient and archaic, thus, could have been already superseded by modern technological developments, some contemporary locations may help clarify. Robert Orsi's collection of essays on New York and other US cities tells us that the urban landscape does not only provide a backdrop – now more cosmopolitan and postmodern – of the religions therein. It also shapes these religions and their practices.[10] The study on Haitian Vodou tells of dislocation of the immigrants from Haiti, but also of the discovery of new sacred spaces in the bustling alleys of New York. The same observation is made of the Cuban Catholic shrine of Our Lady of Charity in Miami or a Hindu temple in Washington, DC. I may add – from personal experience working among Filipinos in these places – the *Santacruzan* in Manhattan or *Simbang Gabi* in all main Catholic churches in any US City. Religions have not retreated to some private realm. These celebrations are publicly held for all to see and participate in. *Santacruzan* re-enacts the religious-cultural ritual-turned-beauty pageant in Philippine towns and villages commemorating the finding of the holy cross by Helena of Constantinople. Along Manhattan's Fifth Avenue, a *Reyna Elena* clad in medieval gown and her small boy, Constantine, lead a procession of her royal court composed of other lower 'queens', 'princesses' and their escorts under arches adorned with flowers. *Simbang Gabi* is a series of dawn Masses nine days before Christmas. In cities outside the Philippines these Masses are attended not only by Filipinos, but also their friends from their host countries. As is usually the case at home, ritual food is served in parish halls after such Masses, to the delight of the non-Filipino guests. Participating in any of these celebrations shows the sacralization of the city as it encounters these religions and the urbanization of these otherwise traditional religious practices as it navigates the plural cityscapes.

Some thinkers declare this contemporary revival of religions as the 'resurgence of religion' in the city, the 're-enchantment of the world'. 'God is back',[11] some writers proclaim. Did God leave in the first place? This assertion still harks back to the secularization theories which sidelined the God-discourse at the coming of modernity and returned in its wake in postmodern times. This might be true of the European experience, but such a model does not hold water for the rest of world. The sociologist José Casanova rightly observes that 'as the rest of the world modernizes, people are not becoming more secular like us, but are becoming more religious – or, actually, they are becoming simultaneously both more secular and more religious, which of course only confuses our binary categories. But once it becomes obvious that the secularization of Europe is, comparatively speaking, rather exceptional, the old theory that explained Europe's secularity in terms of its modernity is no longer plausible.'[12]

The European experience only appears to be a local and singular phenomenon, thus, not universal. Western secularization theories, in fact, continuously fail to explain Asian, African, Pacific or Latin American worlds which endlessly burst with multi-religious fervor and practices regardless of their location in the so-called Western categories of pre-modern, modern and post-modern phases. In these non-Western contexts, immersed as they are in pluralist and multi-religious universes, what the West calls a 'resurgence' or 'revival' of spirituality and religions in postmodernity is, in fact, the usual state of affairs. There is nothing new to this phenomenon. It has always been this way ever since.

I would like to apply the above theoretical considerations on religion and modernity unto a specific context – Manila – considered to be one of the world's megacities. With a relatively small land area, it is densely occupied by 13 million people (out of 100 million-plus all over the country). While daytime and night time populations vary, it is estimated that 42,857 people live in every one square kilometre (or 111,002 per square mile) making it the world's most densely populated city.[13] With this huge mass of people vying for limited opportunities, one can easily guess the consequent social, economic and cultural issues, e.g., homelessness, traffic problems, garbage management, unemployment, hunger and disease, poor social services, etc. While sleek shopping centres and exclusive 'gated communities' of the elite and upper middle classes paint a picture of a bustling megacity, more than 500,000 households are informal settlers (derogatively called 'squatters'). According to the latest statistics, Manila has around 93-95% percent Christian population, mostly Roman Catholic. The rest (5-7%) are Muslims, Buddhists and other faiths. Let me forward two observations on the practice of the Christian religion on the ground on two levels – among the grassroots and on the level of the institutional church.

II Faith Life among the Grassroots

Among the grassroots communities in the megacity, the practice of religion is often the only psychological resource for one's survival. Far from their traditional family networks in the provinces, they cling to religious practices learned from early childhood. Popular religiosity abounds in the megacities not only among Roman Catholics, but also among evangelical and charismatic churches. I surmise it is the same with Islam and other faiths practiced among the grassroots. The phenomenon of local and 'practical Islam' is a negotiation between the long-held fundamental tenets of the vast Islamic world and their adaptation to their local contexts, especially those farthest from Islamic centres of learning.[14] With so many believers and only a few imams, pastors or priests, people on the ground are left to their own creativity in the practice of their religion in order to cope with everyday urban struggles.

Let me focus on Catholic practices at the grassroots since this is the only location I am most familiar with, but is also the religion of the majority in Manila. How do we explain the practice of popular religiosity among the people?[15] Different interpretations from Asian thinkers are used to explain this phenomenon. Let me mention three readings.[16] Jaime Bulatao's 'split-level Christianity'[17] argues that Filipinos have been Christianized but not evangelized, thus, explains the persistence of their pre-Christian animistic beliefs and other discordant moral attitudes in their Christian life. This co-existence of dual moral standards but also dual religiosities (e.g., beliefs in spirits, the need to appease the gods through offerings, etc.) signals 'split-level consciousness' that needs to be overcome if we want authentic evangelization. This same narrative has been adopted by the Catholic hierarchy. Though it also fosters popular religious practices within its controlled universe, supervised as it is by doctrinal guardians, it also holds that these practices need to be purified, corrected or directed towards proper liturgical norms in order to avoid superstition and syncretistic mixtures with local cultures not compatible with Christianity. Such a view is founded on the belief that a 'pure' religion or a monolithic worldview exists. It assumes that if a person accepts one worldview, he or she will totally abandon the other. One who does not do so is not integrated and complete. With psychological categories applied into the theological field, Christians are seen as schizophrenic, socially displaying their bipolar tendencies.

The second optic used to interpret the same phenomenon is the notion of 'hyphenated Christianity' advanced by Peter Phan, a US-based Vietnamese theologian.[18] Reacting to the first lens, Phan argues that religions in Asia are not monolithic nor should aim to be one; it is open to double belonging. One can be a Christian and Asian at the same time without granting primacy to any pole of the binary. According to Phan, there are three phases in the encounter between Christianity and Asian cultures: first is the colonial imposition of Western Christianity (primacy of Christianity); second is syncretistic projects of Matteo Ricci and Robert de Nobili (primacy of Asian cultures); and lastly, through the influence of Vatican II, is Asian-Christian 'hyphenated' existence where both Asianess and Christian-ness cross-fertilize each other. Against Bulatao's lens, this mixture of religious beliefs and sensibilities should not be seen as a malady that needs to be healed through catechises but a natural dynamics of all cultural encounters.

The third interpretative lens critiques the second. Albert Bagus Laksana,[19] an Indonesian philosopher, thinks that the concept of *double belonging* is too 'conscious' a project of Church leaders, say, from the directives of Vatican II, as Phan wanted to envision it. Actual religious-cultural encounters on the ground do not have this programmatic exchanges. They just happen because everyday life makes it happen and, in the process, they mutually borrow from each other. Laksana thinks that Asians live *complex religious identities* toward some type of hybrid Christianity. Complex religious identities come in many forms: multi-religious shared pilgrimage sites; prayer services from different religious traditions; statues of saints or Buddha co-existing side by side on family altars; offering of food on tombs of ancestors on All Souls' Day, etc. Believers do not have qualms of conscience in moving from one religious tradition to the other or of belonging to all of them altogether. Purists, mostly coming from the hierarchical leaders of different religions, condemn this as syncretism or superstition, but it is all that ordinary people have.

This is also how any cultural interaction happens as I have also argued elsewhere.[20] Be it in cultural customs, theologies or religious practice, it is the grassroots communities – not the cultural virtuosos or religious luminaries – who decide which elements of their everyday religious-cultural encounters shall be assimilated or modified, adopted or subverted, consented to or resisted. Be it in urban or rural contexts – religions thrive, mix, accommodate or modify themselves in the context of everyday lives of peoples. The more encounters, the more fusion, thus, the richer the religious practices become. The city and cosmopolitan centres because of its location vigorously allow for this multifaceted fusion making religions more open to the experiences of the other.

We are back to our original question: Has religion evacuated from the modern city as the secularization theories predicted? No. On the contrary, because of its location, religions are made possible to co-exist and flourish, not because the gods have come back with a vengeance after being eclipsed by Enlightenment, but because it has always been this way ever since.

III The Institutional Church and Public Religion

The second observation is the theological gap between the institutional Church the proverbial 'person on the pew'. The Catholic Church in the Philippines and elsewhere pursues a robust theological agenda as can be found in its documents and pronouncements. There are designated church structures and functionaries – bishops, priests, religious and lay leaders – to implement its programs patterned as it is from Vatican directives and local authorities. On the surface, people mimic the gestures in all sincerity. But on the ground, they appropriate the doctrines as their own contexts allow. Actually, the old Latin dictum operates here: '*Quidquid recipitur secundum modum recipientis recipitur*' (Whatever is received, is received according to the capacity of the receiver). When asked to account for their religious affiliation, people never deny their institutional belonging. Though some may change denominational allegiances at one time or another, they still remain in the institutional fold especially during the crucial stages of their lives, e.g., baptism, marriage, death, and their attendant rites and rituals.

Despite its problems, the institutional Church in Manila still serves as the main institutional resource for survival. With the government system not delivering on its social and economic services, the Church comes in as an alternative source – sometimes literally – for people's concrete needs such as housing, poverty alleviation, drainage, youth programs, women protection and empowerment, refuge from political harassment, etc. That is why savings mobilization of the Grameen banking type, Basic Ecclesial Communities, religious congregations that take care of vulnerable population (PWDs, abused women, homeless persons, malnourished children, etc.) abound, providing an alternative resource to a dysfunctional government that cannot cope with the demands of its population.

Ministering to a community that lives around a garbage dump for two decades now, I have been often asked by visitors from abroad: 'What does the government do about it?' The answer is 'nothing'. More recently, in the context of a violent populist government, some sectors of the Church have become the only institutional protection of families whose fathers and sons have been killed by President Duterte's 'war on drugs'. The families and communities they have left behind have nowhere to go – the police, supposed to protect the citizens, are killing them with impunity; the courts are being filled with pro- administration justices; the legislature as well dances to the president;s tune. The Church institution alone provides an alternative haven for security, protection and survival.

Beyond internal relations, the institutional Church has to negotiate with its external 'others'. The sociologist Jose Casanova has ably examined the phenomenon of public religion: 'Religion in the 1980s 'went public' in a dual sense. It entered the 'public sphere' and gained, thereby, 'publicity'. Various 'publics' – the mass media, social scientists, professional politicians, and the 'public at large' – suddenly began to pay attention to religion. The unexpected public interest derived from the fact that religion, leaving its assigned place in the private sphere, had thrust itself into the public arena of moral and political contestation.'[21] Reacting to the privatization of religion by secularization theories, Casanova thinks that religions have been de-privatized and has to account itself to its 'public', to the issues that society sees as important.

One question: how does the institutional Catholic Church in the Philippines position itself vis-à-vis democratic and development issues? The reactions we observe are far from monolithic. The positions we present here come from what one author calls the 'religious elite' related to its institutional structures.[22] The first response is *defensive reaction*. Some democratic and social development agenda like the changing views on gender, abortion, divorce, women empowerment or LGBT issues are most likely to be met with fierce conservative reactions by the institutional church. For instance, the Catholic Bishops' Conference of the Philippines (CBCP) is quite advanced on justice issues against government corruption, but not on family and life issues. Some Church religious leaders are even willing to collaborate with corrupt politicians who uphold the Catholic agenda on family planning and contraception. The second reaction is *democratic preservation*. There is a significant portion of the religious elite that engages politics not in pursuance of issues through party affiliation, but in the preservation of democratic processes like elections. Proclaiming to be neutral, these religious leaders lead their parishioners to be election watchdogs as they try to be inclusive in order not to polarize relationships with the majority of their constituents who find themselves on the opposite side of the political issues. The third response is *comprehensive mobilization*. These sectors of the religious elite pursue clear democratic and development agenda in terms of issues like human rights to housing, comprehensive family planning to gender equality, etc. This makes possible long-term alliances with secular actors, but also the possibility of being censured by the conservative religious hierarchy.

IV Conclusion

Far from the retreat of the divine in globalized megacities, religions in their private and public forms are quite palpable in all nooks and corners of the urban centres. Most often it is a mixture of formal liturgical ritual and popular piety, of Catholic doctrine and pre-animistic practices, the use of amulets or music of New Age inspiration and Marian hymns or scapulars, which many ordinary people practice in the most spontaneous manner without being perturbed by some guilt of harbouring unorthodox belief or syncretic accommodation. Religion in the megacities thrives because it serves as resource for people's everyday survival. The institutional religion, for its part, shows more ambivalence in its position vis-à-vis people's religious practices and other social forces. On the one hand, the Church institution can curtail people's expression of faith by enthroning some practices and denigrating others. On the other hand, it can also provide an alternative haven to the cruel and oppressive political and economic system that dominates the lives of the poor. On the one hand, some sectors of the institution impose a defensive agenda against the global democratic and development forces; on the other hand, other sectors continually dialogue with these new tasks and challenges. The act of living the faith – practiced reflexively in our times – is still considered a source of well-being (or what Christians call 'salvation') within the complex problems and opportunities of the megacities.

Notes

1. C. Wright Mills, *The Sociological Imagination* (London: Oxford University Press, 1959), 33.
2. Peter Berger, *The Sacred Canopy: Elements of a Sociological Theory of Religion* (1967), 134.
3. Peter Berger, *The Rumor of Angels* (Garden City, NY: Doubleday Books. 1969).
4. Cf. Robert Fuller, *Spiritual but not Religious: Understanding Unchurched America* (Oxford: Oxford University Press, 2001); Grace Davie, *Religion in Britain since 1945: Believing Without Belonging* (Oxford: Blackwell, 1994).
5. Cf. Daniel Franklin Pilario, 'Is Asia a Post-religional Society? The Post-religional Paradigm and its Others,' *Horizonte* 13, No. 37 (2015): 279-318.
6. Robert Bellah, *Religion in Human Evolution: From the Paleolithic to the Axial Age* (Cambridge, MA: Harvard University Press, 2011).
7. Mary Hancock and Smirit Srivinas, 'Spaces of Modernity: Religion and the Urban in Asia and Africa,' *International Journal of Urban and Regional Research* 32.2 (2008): 617-630.
8. Robert Bellah, *Religion in Human Evolution* (Cambridge, MA: Harvard University
9. Rodney Stark, *The Rise of Christianity: A Sociologist Reconsiders History* (Princeton, NJ: Princeton University Press, 1996), 10.
10. Robert Orsi, ed., *Gods in the City: Religion and the American Urban Landscape* (Bloomington, IN: Indiana University Press, 1999).
11. John Mickelthwait and Arian Wooldridge, *God is Back: How the Global Revival of Faith is Changing the World* (London: Penguin, 2010); Titus Hjelm, *Is God Back? Reconsidering the New Visibility of Religion* (London: Bloombury, 2015).
12. Jose Casanova, 'Exploring the Postsecular: Three Meanings of the 'Secular' and their Possible Transcendence,' in *Habermas and Religion*, ed. Craig Calhon (London: Polity Press, 2013), 45.
13. 'Manila Population 2018,' in http://worldpopulationreview.com/world-cities/manila-population/ (accessed Nov. 06, 2018).
14. Roy Ellen Ellen, 'Social theory, Ethnography and the Understanding of Practical Islam in South-East Asia,' *Islam in South-East Asia*, ed. M.B. Hooker (Leiden: E.J. Brill, 1983), 51-91.
15. For other studies, see Jayeel Cornelio, *Being Catholic in Contemporary Philippines: Young Catholics Interpreting Religion* (London: Routledge, 2016); Manuel Sapitula, 'Marian Piety and Modernity: Perpetual Help Devotion as Popular Religion in the Philippines,' *Philippine Studies: Historical and Ethnographic Viewpoints* 62, No. 3-4 (2014): 399-424. 16. Cf. Daniel Franklin Pilario, 'Catholics,' in *The Edinburgh Companions to Global Christianity, Vol. 4: East and Southeast Asia*, ed. Kenneth Ross (London: Oxford University Press, [forthcoming]).
17. Jaime Bulatao, *Split-Level Christianity* (Quezon City: Ateneo de Manila University, 1966).
18. Peter Phan, *Christianity with an Asian Face* (Marynoll, NY: Orbis, 2003).

19. Albertus Bagus Laksana, 'Multiple Religious Belonging or Complex Identity? An Asian Way of Being Religious,' *The Oxford Handbook of Asian Christianity* (New York: Oxford University Press,

2014), 493-599.

20. Daniel Franklin Pilario, 'The Craft of Contextual Theologies,' *Hapag: An Interdisciplinary Theological Journal* 1, no. 1 (2004): 5-39.

21. Jose Casanova, *Public Religion in the Modern World* (Chicago: Chicago University Press, 1994), 3.

22. Here we follow the data and categories of David Buckley, 'Catholicism's Democratic Dilemma: Varieties of Public Religion in the Philippines,' *Philippine Studies: Historical and Ethnographic Viewpoints* 62, No. 3-4 (2014): 313-339.

Globalisation, Urbanisation, and the Common Good

LINDA HOGAN

Globalisation has changed the nature of contemporary economic and political life and has created new ethical challenges. In this context the exponential growth of cities and the trajectory of urbanisation not only creates new social, political and economic challenges, but it also magnifies the difficulties associated with creating just, inclusive and equitable political and economic structures. The fact of urbanisation raises, in an acute way, the question of how to live well in the midst of intense diversity. Thus, the question of how cities can contribute to managing pluralism, while also promoting social cohesion, is a crucial one for contemporary society. Building a life in common is a vital task, and must be grounded in the integrity of cultures, traditions and life-worlds.

That we live in the first genuinely global age is something of which one is deeply aware. This awareness is evidenced by the fact that the language of globalisation helps express the nature of our everyday lives. Its usage is no longer limited to the technical worlds of academia or policy-making, rather it has resonance in the wider social context. Referring both to the compression of the world and the intensification of consciousness of the world as a whole, globalisation describes a peculiar interplay of global and local whereby, as Giddens points out, local happenings are shaped by events occurring many miles away and vice versa.[1] Developments in global capitalism and culture, combined with the phenomenal success of technology, especially in the realm of communications, together create an experience of social and political life that is not only novel, but which is invigorating for its beneficiaries. Yet while the term is commonplace, the definition of globalisation and the extent to which it is a new phenomenon has been the subject of extensive debate.

I Globalisation and its Impacts

Debates about the nature and impact of contemporary forms of globalisation are complex and highly charged. They involve disputes about the distinctiveness of the late twentieth-century wave of globalisation relative to earlier waves; about the extent to which economic globalisation provides opportunities for development and inclusion, or whether it propels impoverishment and exclusion; and about whether globalisation can be directed towards the global common good (however that is defined), or whether its forces inevitably undermine forms of solidarity that underpin a commitment to global goods and good. Through the 1990s and 2000s debates about the nature of globalisation and its impact tended to be premised on an account of globalisation that was primarily economic. Through this period, hyper-globalists pointed to the benefits that would accrue from the expansion of trade and investment flows, the integration of financial markets, the voluminous global trade in currencies and the nomadic practices of trans-national corporations.[2] Critics, on the other hand, were concerned not only about the ambivalent economic impacts of globalisation on different populations world-wide, but also about the political and cultural impact of this unprecedented integration.[3] The subsequent populist backlash against globalisation, expressed in the election of Donald Trump as President of the USA and by the decision of the UK to exit the European Union was anticipated by few, but has come to define politics in many parts of the globe in the last few years. Of course, globalisation has not only impacted the economic sphere, since in addition to economic flows, one can see the remarkable growth of transnational social movements, of global civil society, and of new global institutions as evidence of an increasingly interconnected world.

Whatever one's position on these debates, it is nonetheless clear that globalisation has changed the nature of contemporary economic and political life to such an extent that previously national concerns have been transformed into international ones. Additionally, this unprecedented international integration has created ostensibly new phenomena, namely challenges that can only be tackled in an international context and goods that can only be sought and secured through global political action. Thus, daily we encounter challenges that no government can successfully deal with alone, challenges of environmental degradation, nuclear and chemical proliferation, migration, terrorism. Beneath these challenges are often questions about equality and justice, also issues that are embedded in this globalized and globalizing context, even if the manifestation of these challenges is often decidedly local. Moreover, in the midst of all of this there persists a fragile system of global institutions, attempting to grapple with these issues, through international governance bodies, treaties and accords.

II The Ethical Challenges of Globalisation

The ethical challenges that are posed by this account of our political milieu are manifold. Critics have drawn attention to the negative effects of unregulated or unfairly regulated markets, of the consolidation economic activity in the developing world and of currency speculation, in many parts of the globe. The ever-increasing economic disparity between North and South as well as the shameful impoverishment of many countries are also seen by many as the inevitable, but unacceptable by-products of globalisation. In response, politicians, civil society activists and academics around the world have argued for an ethical globalisation, that is a form of economic and political integration which is subject to ethical considerations, and that respects all human rights, that is economic, social and cultural rights as well as political and civil rights. The phrase 'ethical globalisation' has been controversial, since many anti-globalisation activists argue that it is a tautology. Nonetheless its advocates argue that it represents the best chance for individuals and communities around the world to secure livelihoods characterised by decency and dignity, rather than destitution.[4] It points to the need to pursue forms of globalisation that serve rather than undermine human development, and this means that the impetus of economic globalisation needs to be moderated and governed by ethical principles, a task that is growing more urgent each day.

Globalisation has created many new global challenges, not least of which are the challenges associated with urbanisation. Although it has a range of causative factors, the contemporary drive towards urbanisation is undoubtedly propelled primarily by globalisation. Moreover, the exponential growth of cities and the trajectory of urbanisation not only creates new social, political and economic challenges, but it also magnifies the difficulties associated with creating just, inclusive and equitable political and economic structures. Indeed, the fact of urbanisation raises, in an acute way, the question of how to live well, in the midst of this intensity of social relationships, and amongst neighbours whose values, commitments and practices I do not share. In this context the ambivalent nature of globalisation is again in view, for in addition to driving integration, globalisation has also set in train a number of contradictory processes, including a trajectory of fragmentation, seen in the forces of nationalism, identity politics and religious fundamentalism.[5] Yet the question of how cities can contribute to managing this pluralism, while also promoting social cohesion, is a crucial one for contemporary society. Moreover, for those concerned with the position of religion there is a further question of the role that religious communities can play in advancing such cohesion, and whether religion will be part of the problem or part of the solution.

III Urbanisation and Pluralism

The challenge of living well in the midst of cultural and ethical pluralism is one with which humanity has grappled in a myriad of contexts and in every age. However, the mobility associated with globalisation has created contexts in which we see more intense levels of ethnic, cultural and religious pluralism than heretofore, and this is also amplified through the complementary drive towards urbanisation. It is present in an intense and exaggerated form in the great global cities of the world such as New York, Los Angeles, London, Singapore, Hong Kong, Mexico City, Mumbai, Beijing. Many of these cities already are, and others will become, hyper-diverse. They will be multi-lingual, multi-racial and multi-cultural and multi-religious. In addition, as Ignatieff notes, 'in post-imperial globalisation, the once dominant and once subordinate races live together in hyper-diverse global cities, former colonialists and the colonized cheek by jowl …'.[6] But others cities, for example Beijing, Mumbai and Mexico City, will become larger, more densely populated, but will draw populations in from the surrounding regions and nations. Therefore, although they will be diverse in different ways (in terms of background, skills or language), they will likely be made up of peoples who mostly (but not exclusively) share cultural, racial and religious backgrounds. As a result, the issue in these cities will not be the hyper-diversity of post-imperial immigration, but rather the challenge of the presence of minorities amongst larger and more densely homogeneous populations.[7]

Thus, managing a pluralism that embraces different ways of life will be different in contexts of hyper-diversity as opposed to contexts of cultural and religious majoritarianism. Much of the ethical reflection in this context has been focussed on the extent to which shared moral values can be generated in the midst of this pluralism, and about the extent to which such shared values can establish the parameters of the common good, in local and global contexts, in this era of globalisation. These are the parameters of the question that are considered in the *Humanity on the Move* report. However, of equal consequence is the question of how and whether the universal principles of equal dignity and respect prevail in the local, mostly urban contexts where diverse communities live side by side, and where the negotiation between multiple ethnic and religious traditions, and the liberal values of equal dignity and rights is part of the experience of everyday life.

IV Constructing a Common Ground
In this regard, Michael Ignatieff's *Ordinary Virtues Moral Order in a Divided World* argues that what enables communities to live successfully side by side, if not together, is not the universalist languages of human rights or equality (these he argues are the languages of liberal elites and of states) but rather it is what he calls the everyday virtues of tolerance, forgiveness, trust and resilience. These, he suggests are the glue that makes the multicultural experiment work. They are the moral operating system in global cities and obscure shanty towns alike. In addition to these ordinary virtues, which he argues are present in diverse communities and traditions across the globe, a thin moral consensus, mandating limited trust, non-violence and co-operation is necessary to keep a global city functioning.[8]

Thus, a common ground cannot be created by suppressing or supplanting the competing traditional familial, ethnic or religious allegiances or values into which people are born. Primary loyalties cannot be suppressed, rather they need to be harnessed, and balanced with the secondary affiliations in order to make a multicultural city, and indeed a multicultural world, functioning.[9] Nor do these issues arise only in contexts of hyper-diversity. The question of managing pluralism is equally important, indeed one might say even more crucial, in contexts of cultural and religious homogeneity in which are present small-scale minority groups. Whether in contexts of hyper-diversity or of cultural homogeneity, the common good is frequently and often improperly invoked to justify restrictions on pluralism and minority rights. However, the common good cannot be conceptualised in terms of a trade-off between the rights of minorities and those of majorities but rather, the common good ought to be concerned with 'construing the relationship of the individual to society so that the limits and possibilities of both individual and communal well-being are preserved, and in which the appropriate responsibilities and obligations that exist among individuals are clarified and articulated.'[10] The common good concerns the harmonisation of different values in the attainment of a just and cohesive society, and this harmonisation is as important in contexts where one tradition dominates, as it is in contexts of hyper-diversity.

So how then can we go about building a life in common? What kind of approach to the interplay of different cultural and religious values will be most productive, whether the pluralism is wide and deep, or minimal and marginal? Building such a life in common must be grounded in an appreciation of the integrity of the distinct moral and religious traditions and in a desire to build discursive bridges across these traditions, in the expectation that a durable consensus on shared values can be established. The most persuasive responses to the challenges of living well together will only be found through multiple, inclusive, tradition-thick, cross-cultural, multi-religious engagements and dialogue.

What shape this deliberation and dialogue should take and what it will take to create the spaces in which such dialogue can take place? Even our local conversations about human dignity and flourishing are now shaped by the irreducible plurality of human experience, including religious experience, and this will only become more pronounced in the future. Thus, our political cultures, even, especially at the municipal and national levels must also have the capacity to facilitate such intercultural and interreligious exchange. Crucial in this regard is the capacity of religious traditions to be part of this deliberative process, a process in which there is mutual respect for the convictions, including the moral and religious convictions, of the other, and in which there is a mutual appreciation of the ethical values embedded in these discrete and varied traditions. Indeed, since religious pluralism has become entangled with the politics of fear, it is more vital than ever that religious traditions are to the fore in the process of building a municipal politics focused on the global common good.

Notes

1. Anthony Giddens, *The Consequences of Modernity* (Oxford: Polity Press, 1990), 64.

2. See Thomas Friedman, *The Lexus and the Olive Tree* (New York: Farrar, Straus & Giroux, 1999) and *The World is Flat* (New York: Farrar, Straus & Giroux, 2005).

3. Dani Rodik, *Has Globalization Gone Too Far?* (New York: Columbia University Press, 1997) represented an early critique of the hyper-globalist trajectory, as did the work of former World Bank economist Joseph Stiglitz with his influential *Globalisation and its Discontents* (New York, W. W. Norton & Co, 2002). See also Dani Rodik's *The Globalization Paradox: Democracy and the Future of the World Economy* (New York: W. W. Norton & Co., 2011).

4. Mary Robinson, 'An Ethical Human-rights Approach to Globalization,' *Peace Review* 16: 1 March 2004, 13-17.

5. Zigmud Bauman coins the neologism 'glocalisation to capture this ambiguity. See 'On Glocalization: or Globalization for Some, Localization for Some Others' *Thesis Eleven*, 54(1), 1998, 37–49.

6. Michael Ignatieff, *Ordinary Virtues Moral Order in a Divided World*, (Cambridge MA.: Harvard University Press, 2017) 14.

7. See Saskia Sassen's *The Global City* (Princeton NJ: Princeton University Press, 1991), for a comprehensive discussion of these points.

8. Ignatieff op. cit. 45

9. Ibid., 202

10. David Hollenbach, *The Common Good and Christian Ethics* (Cambridge: Cambridge University Press, 2002), 192.

Part Four: The Praxis of Creating Humane Spaces

Liberating Urban Development and the South African Church: A Critical Reflection in Conversation with David Korten and Gustavo Gutierrez

STEPHAN DE BEER

In this article I reflect on (post)apartheid cities, from the perspective of spatial (re)segregation, homelessness and precarious housing. I submit that the Church will find herself increasingly isolated from the growing discontent of the urban marginalized, unless it embraces all four generations of development, as outlined by David Korten, whilst rooting herself in a deep commitment to integral liberation, as defined by Gustavo Gutierrez. I conclude by discerning and suggesting seven urgent imperatives for theological action.

I The (Post)apartheid City

The spatial injustices of the past remain etched on the South African urban landscape. Whereas forced removals and apartheid legislation displaced black South Africans before the 1990s, gentrification of inner city neighbourhoods, and sprawling urban informal settlements, continue to displace, or marginalize, mostly black South Africans. The majority of our population does not have proximity or access to urban opportunity.

Today, re-segregation has become evident, not only in urban public schools, but also in new forms of economic segregation separating middle-classes and wealthy gated communities from urban informal settlements and backyard shack dwellers. There are some exceptions, where the starkness of the segregated city is 'disrupted' through the suburbanization of homelessness,[1] or the occupation of land and buildings in strategic urban places. In addition to the perpetuation of socio-spatial segregation, many young black South Africans have grown disillusioned with the rainbow of Mandela, suggesting that reconciliation was never coupled with justice.[2] The cry for land, a right to the city, and basic human dignity – still elusive for way too two decades after democracy – is becoming more pronounced, and increasingly impatient.

II Urbanization, Housing and Homelessness

By 2050 almost 1,3 billion people will live in African cities today, 43% of Africa's urban dwellers live in informal settlements.[3] Both rural-urban and trans-national migration fast-tracks the pace of urbanization across the continent. It is similar in (post)apartheid South Africa.

The Gauteng City-Region, in which both Johannesburg and the City of Tshwane are located, has a population of 14,7 million people.[4] The City of Tshwane, the location from which I reflect theologically, has around 3,3 million inhabitants,[5] with Pretoria at its core. The person responsible for housing in our city said it will take 40 years to address our current housing backlog, not even taking into account the projected growth rates of our city.[6] 13,1% of all households in South Africa live in informal dwellings whilst that is true for 19% of all households in the Gauteng City-Region.[7] An estimated 200,000 people are homeless on the streets of South Africa. In the City of Tshwane there are more than 6,200 street homeless people, of which more than 1,200 are over the age of 65 years.[8]

Considering the pace of urban migration, the slowness (and incapacity) in addressing challenges of precarious housing and homelessness, and the seeming inability of African cities to get their heads and hearts around the pace of urban expansion, demands for urban infrastructure, and increasing inequalities, raise critical questions.

III The Migrant, Homeless Jesus in the Urban Dungeons: A Question of Faith and Theology

The restlessness of the urban poor in our context is growing. Yet, the Church locates itself, according to Vuyani Vellem, not *in* the dungeons of modern-day urban enslavement,[9] but *on top* of the dungeons, too often participating in repressing vulnerable people. If our theological work fails to engage the migrant, homeless Jesus – who makes himself a slave in the dungeons,[10] with the urban poor – then our theological work is irrelevant to the majority of urban people.

Urban development conversations in our context seldom have a theologian in the room. This is symptomatic both of dominant development discourse's negative or ignorant views of faith-based action, but also of the lack of theological rigour and savvy to engage urban complexity well. Stuck in our theological or religious silos, we seldom work in transdisciplinary ways, either to participate in constructing the city, or to prepare (read: re-educate) ourselves for an urban future.

If the South African church fails to express itself in radical solidarity with the urban margins, except through escapist ritual, Jesus does not necessarily do the same. In discerning and connecting to the migrant, homeless Jesus *in* the urban dungeons, we will start engaging issues of land and housing, water and sanitation, street homelessness and informal settlement upgrading. Jesus amongst the urban poor cries out for that.

IV Liberating Urban Development: Deepening Urban Impact
In this section I propose an embrace of Korten's four generations of development, and Gutierrez's notion of 'integral liberation', in order to liberate urban development and deepen urban impact.

Korten's four generations
David Korten speaks of four generations of development, gradually shifting from relief work (first generation) addressing short-term needs, to community development (second generation) creating infrastructure; and from advocacy and policy work (third generation) focusing on structural changes, to building local, regional and global movements working for long-term political change (fourth generation).[11] Ignatius Swart[12] advocates for a fourth generation approach by Churches engaging development in South Africa. Instead of focusing on relief only, or being co-opted into state welfare or development programmes, the Church will then collaborate with local and global social movements, working for systemic change both at regional and global level.

Korten's model is helpful for assessing own developmental approaches, but also to provoke deeper journeys, never negating the importance of relief and community development, but attending more intentionally to structural concerns. This article emphasizes the necessity for liberating urban development – both the process of liberating our urban praxis, as well as ensuring that our praxis mediates deep, integral liberation.

Gutierrez' integral liberation

I propose Gutierrez's 'integral liberation' as the purpose of our developmental engagement with urban poverty. He radicalises our understanding of development, not only mediating personal freedom through salvation from personal sin; or interpersonal freedom through humanizing relations of race, class, gender, or sexuality; but also mediating liberation in a socio-economic-spatial-political sense. I include spatial liberation as part of Gutierrez's third category and add environmental liberation, drawing on Boff's[12] insistence that the cry of the poor and the earth are similar cries, caused by patriarchal oppression.

I suggest as the role of Church- and faith-based communities, and as criteria by which to measure their contribution, the mediation of multiple freedoms: personal; interpersonal; socio-economic-spatial-political; and environmental. A great contribution to faith-based engagement with urban development would be to develop concrete indicators to measure in how far multiple freedoms are being mediated.

V The Urban Church in the City of Tshwane

The urban Church in Tshwane, with exceptions, practices a first or second generation approach to urban development, if there is any engagement. Faith-based advocacy or rights work, as expressions of a third or fourth generation approach to development, is rare. Even more rare is the occurrence of South African Church participating in local or global social movements for systemic change. For many years I participated in an ecumenical movement[14] responding to rapid socio-demographic changes in the inner city of Pretoria, since 1993. In organic ways we journeyed with local communities, discerning the cries of particularly vulnerable groups, and the face of Jesus in them. Over the years, it created a presence and a number of *small intentional communities alongside particularly vulnerable people* in the city: women at-risk, vulnerable girl children; or homeless people living with chronic mental illness. In these communities, people who were vulnerable, violated or abused, and homeless, found home, and started to access the resources of the city. We were taught the power of small communities to mediate the sustainable integration of vulnerable people into the big city. We discovered the importance of creating access as a ministry of opening doors, rolling away stones,[15] and mediating freedoms. Small, caring communities became communities of justice, uncovering 'the thief'[16] who caused their vulnerability to start with.

In 1998 the same ecumenical movement created *a social housing company*[17] offering access to affordable housing but also proximity to urban resources. It engaged in the work of *advocacy and awareness-raising*, with and on behalf of different groups it was in solidarity with. Some interventions informed policy and practices, especially in relation to neighbourhood organizing, counter-trafficking work, homelessness advocacy and a demonstration of viable models of social housing. As part of its journey it invested in *building capacity and leadership* of those working with the Foundation. Increasingly it builds leadership capacity of people who are homeless or particularly vulnerable, affirming the agency they themselves practice in spite of the odds stacked against them.

This movement, as an expression of a faith-based urban development response, embraced the first three generations, but could deepen its third generation work and be more intentional about a fourth generation approach. At times its advocacy approach lacked strategic intent and impact, either being too *ad hoc* or not connecting well enough to broader-based movements. In recent times it started to build strategic alliances with other social movements to accelerate its impact in terms of ending homelessness, housing advocacy, and activist education. TLFs longing has always been to mediate fullness of life: disarming the thieves preventing it, and facilitating access to multiple freedoms. I would submit that TLF, and other faith-based communities, would have a liberating impact if they had to embrace Korten's third and fourth generation approaches more deliberately, combining it with a deep awareness and embrace of its own pastorate as being profoundly political.

VI Urgent Imperatives for a (Post)apartheid Urban Theological Agenda

Elsewhere, with Ignatius Swart, we outlined a possible urban public theological agenda for South Africa today.[18] What I do here is different. Based on the thread of this article, I discern specific challenges requiring immediate and urgent theological attention.

1. We have to articulate the illusion of the (post)apartheid city and the on-going pervasiveness of the apartheid city, for faith audiences to understand the wound of the urban marginalized.

2. We need to place the challenge of African urbanization – migration, informality, homelessness, housing, the spatiality of justice, and access to appropriate infrastructure – centre stage in our theological endeavour.

3. We need to discern the migrant, homeless Jesus *in* the urban dungeon; and expose expressions of Church being exploitatively on top of the dungeon.

4. We need to accompany, theologically, homelessness agendas emerging in cities across the country, as well as faith-based (and other) housing approaches seeking to address precarity.

5. We would do well to learn from and collaborate with social movements focusing critically and constructively on land, housing and spatial justice.[19]

6. We need to theologically locate ourselves in all four generations of Korten, but in particular in the third and fourth generations which have not been practised much by the South African urban church: integrating care, community development, advocacy and policy work, and participation in social movements.

7. We need to be re-evangelized into a more integral understanding of salvation as integral liberation.[20] Our faith is indeed political, in its apathy or avoidance of the *polis*; in its presence in the polis; or, indeed, in its more articulate engagement with the concerns of the *polis*. We can practice a liberating politics, inside the urban dungeons; or participate in an oppressive politics on top of the dungeons.

For the urban Church in South Africa to embrace an urban liberationist agenda, would require of theological education to be urbanized and liberated from its anti-urban captivity.[21] If not, the Church would increasingly be irrelevant to the cries of the urban masses. Our salvation is fortunately not in the Church, but in the One who finds himself 'outside the gate',[22] inside the dungeons.

1. S.de Beer & R. Vally, *Pathways out of Homelessness*, (Pretoria: University of Pretoria, 2015), 63-65.
2. M.Van der Merwe, 'Anger and Reconciliation: Lingering Inequality's Impact on Social Cohesion', *Daily Maverick*, 8 November 2016; N.Gous, 'Reconciliation is Impossible Without Redress', *Times Live*, 31 August 2018.
3. S.Parnell & E.Pieterse (eds.), Africa's Urban Revolution, (London: Zed Books, 2014) 1,3, 64.
4. Gauteng City-Region Observatory, The Gauteng City-Region, http://www.gcro.ac.za/, 2018.
5. Municipalities of South Africa, City of Tshwane Metropolitan Municipality, https://municipalities. co.za/demographic/3/city-of-tshwane-metropolitan-municipality, 2018.
6. A personal conversation with Nonto Memela, Group Head: Housing and Human Settlement, in the City of Tshwane Metropolitan Municipality, 25 May 2018.
7. Statistics South Africa, *GHS Series Volume VII: Housing from a human settlement perspective*, Media Release 20 April 2016, http://www.statssa.gov.za/?p=6429
8. S.de Beer & R.Vally, *Pathways out of Homelessness. Research Report*, (Pretoria: University of Pretoria, 2015), 3.
9. V.S. Vellem, 'The Reformed Tradition as Public Theology', *HTS Theological Studies / Teologiese Studies* 69(1), Art. #1371 (Vellem describes urban informal settlements and slums as urban dungeons and modern-day forms of enslavement); K.Cannon, 'Lessons of Liberation in the Struggle for Freedom', in P.Dibeela, P.LenkaBula & V.Vellem (eds.), *Prophet from the south: Essays in honour of Allan Aubrey Boesak*, (Stellenbosch: SUN MeDIA, 2015) 173
10. Cf. Phil.2:5-8
11. D.Korten, *Getting to the 21st Century. Volunteer Action and the Global Agenda*, (West Hartford, CT: Kumarian Press, 1991) 113-132.
12. I.Swart, *The Churches and the Development Debate: Perspectives on a Fourth Generation Approach*, (Stellenbosch: SUN Press, 2006).
13. L.Boff, *Cry of the Earth, Cry of the Poor*, Maryknoll, NY: Orbis 2002).
14. Tshwane Leadership Foundation, http://tlf.org.za/, 2016.
15. Cf. C.Myers, *Who Will Roll Away the Stone? Discipleship Queries for First World Christians*, (Maryknoll, NY: Orbis, 1994), with reference to Mark 16:3.
16. Cf. 'the thief' of John 10:10, hell-bent on preventing access to sharing in the abundance of life God intended.
17. Yeast City Housing, https://www.ych.org.za/home, 2018.
18. I. Swart & S. De Beer, S., Doing Urban Public Theology in South Africa: Introducing a New Agenda, *HTS Theological Studies / Teologiese Studies*, 70(3), Art. #2811, 14 pages. http://dx.doi. org/10.4102/hts.v70i3.2811
19. S. de Beer, Urban Social Movements in South Africa Today: Its Meaning for Theological Education and the Church, *HTS Theological Studies / Teologiese Studies*, 73(3), a4770, 2017 https://doi. org/10.4102/hts.v73i3.4770
20. G. Gutierrez, *A Theology of Liberation*, (Maryknoll, NY: Orbis, 1988), xxxviii-xl.
21. A. Shorter, *The Church in the African City*, (Maryknoll, NY: Orbis, 1991).
22. O. Costas, *Christ Outside the Gate: Mission Beyond Christendom*, (Maryknoll, NY: Orbis, 1982)

The Contribution of Civil Society Organisations to Transformation: Consequences for the Work of NGOs – Misereor

GEORG STOLL

Global trends in population growth, in the development of technology and the economy, as well as the burden on the environment, make far-reaching changes likely in the coming decades. 'Humanity', the virtual collective of all human beings, consequently faces the immense and, in this form, novel task of finding ways to give these changes a 'humane' shape, without previously having a common understanding of what is human or humane. In this task of humane transformation cities have a particular role, both as focal points of global trends and agents of transformation. They have this role because of their great potential actively to shape the approaching changes. Non-governmental organisations such as Misereor must face the challenge of reflecting on their place, their procedures and their structures in the face of these changing parameters.

I The dynamics of global changes

For about 200 years the world population has undergone exponential growth, which has pushed the number of human beings living on (and depending on) the earth to constant new records. Each of the recent generations has seen a doubling of global population. Even if in the meantime this curve has flattened off and in this century will probably reach a ceiling, this ceiling will be at a hitherto unprecedented level of nine to eleven million. Moreover this growth is not even across regions, and so brings about not only global changes in factors such as the load on the ecosystem; it also

103

creates pressure for change in structures and balances of power in and between the various regions of the world. This can currently be seen in the shrinking geopolitical influence of Europe and North America and the growing political weight of Asian countries, especially China. Africa, the region with far and away the highest population growth rate, will in the near future have considerably more weight in world politics.

A further factor with high potential to change the situation is the composition of the population. Whereas increasing growth rates initially give greater weight to younger sectors of the population, falling growth rates shift the population balance, at least temporarily, towards the older generations. Such differences can have considerable political effects, starting with their impact on social policy (e.g. education, work force and health care), on a society's mobility and capacity for innovation, and even on the style of its politics. And between states relations and balances of forces also change when a younger population faces an ageing one.

The high speed of technical developments and their application in the economy is a further factor in global changes. The scale and complexity of global networking that is now possible are due essentially to this process. A good example is the use of technology in global markets. High frequency trading using algorithms, which has a turnover several times the value of annual global economic output, would have seemed like science fiction only a few decades ago. Such developments create all sorts of insecurity. They are perceived as processes that can have enormous consequences (perhaps in the relationship between legitimate democratic politics and large corporations with a transnational reach). On the other hand, such technical developments and their economic value chains are regarded as highly complex and opaque, and so far removed from the understanding and action of one individual. The increasing automation of our use of technology in everyday life, through 'user interfaces', may be convenient – but it also illustrates the degree of dependence and loss of control that can degrade the individual to a 'user'.

A third major trend that produces global changes which are already clearly visible is the continuing extreme pressure on ecological systems and cycles from human activity. The most notable example is climate change as a result of human activity, which so far has continued to advance despite all technological and political efforts. Nevertheless, this is by no means the only area of problematic global environmental changes. The massively disturbed nitrogen cycle and the huge decline in the variety of species are further acute problem areas. The main causes of this crossing of our planet's ecological boundaries can be identified in the area of production as primarily the production of energy from fossil fuels, followed by intensive agriculture – though in the area of consumption these are matched by a steadily rising demand, driven not only by a rising world population but also by increased consumer expectations and unsustainable consumption patterns.

II Cities as the source both of global change and of its transformation

These three linked global trends operate especially in cities and so dominate the current discussion on urbanisation. Although population growth in rural areas on average clearly continues to exceed that in towns, across the world the proportion of people living in towns is increasing. The disproportionate growth of the urban population is a result on the one hand of a continuing inward migration from country to town and on the other of that fact that a good many settlements have themselves grown to the size of small towns. In this way new towns are constantly coming into being, while at the same time existing towns also grow in an autonomous process until they reach the dimensions of megacities with over 10 million inhabitants. The number of these will certainly increase in the coming years. Global population growth is thus taking place mainly in towns despite measures such as space restrictions (and the resulting competition for space), and issues such as traffic density, infrastructure, dependence on external supply for food, diversity of population groups, anonymity, administration, etc. These conditions on the one hand make cities particularly vulnerable to the negative consequences of the two trends already mentioned (in technology and economics, and in the environment), though at the same time they contain a unique potential for a humane shaping of the forthcoming changes.

Cities are not only tending to concentrate living areas and transport systems, but are also becoming the location of choice for economic activities. Manufacturing and commercial enterprises, and educational establishments and research centres, prefer to set up in urban areas or on their outskirts, to take advantage of the availability of a workforce and infrastructure, but also of the potential for innovation of an urban environment. As a result, cities have the potential to develop solutions to the need to provide a growing population with the necessary services and to do so in a way that respects not only local but also global ecological load limits. At the same time cities are also vulnerable to the negative impacts of technological and economic development, such as when the closure of a firm or structural changes lead to huge job cuts, or when wide-ranging technical monitoring systems mean that citizens spend their lives under constant surveillance.

Particularly striking examples of both the vulnerability and the potential of cities have to do with the third transformation trend, global environmental changes. On the one hand cities are going to feel the effects of climate change to a particular degree, through flooding in areas near the coast or through the rise in average temperatures, which in towns are anyway already above the values in the surrounding countryside. On the other hand, cities have a high potential efficiency for using available resources, and these can be exploited, through intelligent building techniques, traffic planning and building controls, to a greater degree than hitherto. In addition, cities are also increasingly bringing their political weight in global environmental issues to bear in international discussions and so increasing the pressure for action by national and international leaders.

III Demands for transformation on an NGO like Misereor
Despite the cliché, the world is not becoming a global village but more of a global city – a city whose inhabitants are markedly diverse, but face common situations and problems that demand cooperation and solidarity. What does that mean for an NGO like Misereor, which since its foundation 60 years ago has been committed to a view of comprehensive development that puts the poor and the poorest of the poor at its heart?

1. Understand development as a common global task
In addition to regional problems, the three major trends mentioned above face all countries with challenges that can only be met if they work together. This situation, reflected notably in the sustainable development goals of Agenda 2030, means for Misereor thinking about North and South together and bearing in mind the specific global responsibilities of our own country. This also means setting ideology on one side and engaging in a critical discussion of existing development models and looking for enduring visions of a good life for all in dialogue with partner organisations in Africa, Asia and Latin America. If it is to be valid for the long-term, this

dialogue about transformation must become part of the daily routine of all concerned.

2. See cities as sites of global development and transformation
The importance of cities comes not only from the fact that the majority of human beings are by now living in cities (and the tendency is for this to continue). It comes also from the fact that cities can act as laboratories for alternative attitudes and techniques beyond their boundaries and become models. For Misereor this means keeping an eye out for such experimental processes that are relevant to the lives of poor city-dwellers. Misereor can promote and publicise such processes.

3. Look at cities not sectorally but as a whole
Many partner organisations work on different social problems in an urban environment, but the connections between the different sets of problems are not always seen. For Misereor this means starting to take a town planner's view and encourage partner organisations to do so as well. It is often only such a view that makes it possible to identify conflicting goals, for example between social and ecological issues, without excluding one side through haste.

4. Include experiences with plurality and diversity
Urban societies face the task of integrating different population groups without denying their distinctiveness. The international community faces a similar task with the challenges of global development and transformation. In this context Misereor can draw on its years of experience in dealing with plurality and diversity and use it in transformative development processes.

5. Take new middle classes seriously as global players
The quantifiable and measurable development successes of the past decades are closely related to the rise of new middle classes, especially in Asia. These middle classes generally live in the growing cities of the region and set the tone for their lifestyle. Because of their increasing influence on economics and politics they play an important role in the future of global development. Misereor, as an NGO with an explicit focus on fighting poverty, must now face the new question of how these new urban middle classes can be brought into an overall strategy for global development.

One of the participants in Misereor's 60th-anniversary conference on cities said, 'If you do not imagine your future someone else will colonise your future.' In the face of the global challenges great imagination is necessary to identify alternative paths to a liveable future. Whether and how these different ideas and paths come together is, however, a question of power relations. Cities, which can be places of exchange and of competition, will play a key role in deciding this.

Translated by Francis McDonagh

Living with Dignity and Peace: Social Mobilization for Housing Rights and the Right to the City

LORENA ZÁRATE

For more than forty years, Habitat International Coalition members have been mobilizing around the world to defend and guarantee ever person's right to a safe place to live with dignity and peace. Our two-legged strategy seeks to strengthen the social actors and processes, while it aims to influence medium and long-term changes through advocacy efforts in public policy, legal frame-work and international agendas. From its origins, our Coalition has been aware of the relevance of coordinating local and national actions with regional and global presence to advance social justice, gender equality and environmental sustainability working with a broad range of actors and institutions.

I Just One World... with Dual Cities

Habitat International Coalition (HIC) is the global, independent and non-profit network for the defence and realization of every person' right to a safe place to live with dignity and peace. Established in 1976 in Vancouver, Canada, within the framework of the first United Nations Conference on Human Settlements (known as Habitat I), it consist today of more than 350 member-organizations in 120 countries, including NGOs, CBOs, professional, research and education institutions, as well as human rights activists working to advance social justice, gender equality and environmental sustainability.

Born during a decade where the environmentalist concern was gaining ground vis-à-vis the imposition of the irrational myth of perpetual growth in a finite planet, HIC emerged to raise awareness of the human rights dimensions and to highlight the need to understand the characteristics and challenges faced by marginalized and impoverished communities. From professionals and academics, to community organizers and faith-based individuals and institutions, hundreds of women and men engaged on long-life commitments to promote human rights and the democratization of their societies. Many among them influenced by the liberation theology and the pedagogy of the oppressed in the context of dictatorships and authoritarian regimes, they joined broad progressive platforms and social movements, and some later became local or national public officials.

The struggle for the promotion, defence and realization of housing and land rights and the right to the city in equitable and peaceful conditions continues to be as necessary and relevant as it was four decades ago. Probably more than ever before, human settlements are today a clear expression of the growing inequality, dispossession, discrimination and violence suffered by increasingly larger sectors of the population, both in the South and in the North, with women and girls being disproportionally affected.

Profit is above the well-being, dignity, needs and rights of people and nature, provoking conflicts, gentrification processes and man-made risks and disasters that cause displacement and evictions of traditional and low-income populations; dual cities of luxury and misery; millions of empty buildings and millions of homeless people and people without a decent place to live; ten-ants suffering inadequate living conditions and that cannot afford to pay the rent; peasants with-out land and land without peasants, subjected to abuses by agro-businesses, mining and other extractive industries and large scale projects; and massive waves of migrants and refugees condemned to violence and stigmatization, both in their home countries and the countries of passing and destination. We see the privatization of public spaces, infrastructure and basic services, vicious cycles of destruction-construction, extreme income concentration and cuts in social spending and 'austerity' policies for the majority, while corporate, authoritarian and criminal powers grow.

According to the UN Special Rapporteur on the Right to Adequate Housing, the value of the global real-estate is about USD 217 trillion and represents nearly 60 percent of all global assets — many unoccupied or underutilized. At the same time, UN-Habitat reports that one third of the global urban population suffers from inadequate living conditions: lack of access to basic services (drinking water and/or sanitation, not to mention energy, waste recollection, and transportation), low structural quality of shelters, overcrowding, dangerous locations, and insecure tenure.

The trend towards population concentration in cities and metropolitan areas is presented as irreversible (our 'urban future'), and as the only desirable and possible way of living. From aphorisms that glorify life in cities and their role in relation to rural areas ('engines of development', 'magnets of hope'), to the apocalyptic denunciation that we are headed towards 'a planet of slums', the predominant narratives seems to be trapped between extreme visions that fail to ex-plain the reality surrounding us. In both cases, very little is said about the structural causes, the responsibilities of the various social actors, the interconnectedness between the urban and rural worlds, or about the hues, challenges and possibilities to tackle these processes.

II International Networking, Local Transformation

For more than forty years HIC members have been actively engaged in challenging paradigms and experimenting with a wide range of alternatives in cities and villages around the world.

Land and Housing Rights, the Social Protection of Habitat and the Right to the City have become crucial relevant pillars of our conceptual, pedagogical and advocacy work at local, national, regional and international level. These are based on understanding i) the right to a place to live as a basic human right for dignity and peace ii) nature as a common good for current and future generations and iii) the city and human settlements as collective creations for more just, democratic, inclusive and sustainable societies.

Our work has focused on: proposals for the inclusion of these perspectives in constitutions and legal frameworks in Bolivia, Brazil, Colombia, Ecuador, France, Mexico and South Africa. We have also been involved in co-designing, and monitoring policies to support collective efforts to create or improve housing and neighbourhood conditions of disadvantaged groups in Angola, Argentina, El Salvador, Guatemala, Nicaragua, Spain, Switzerland and Uruguay. We have challenged regulations that criminalize homeless people and those they help. We denounce and work to prevent forced evictions and other violations of housing and land rights in the Middle East and North Africa.

At the same time, we strive to eliminate all forms of discrimination against women and to implement legislation that guarantees women's

111

habitat rights, including inheritance rights and access to adequate infrastructure and facilities. While challenging gender-based violence and its linkages with the rights to housing, land and the city, our members work to strengthen women's leader-ship at all levels. Co-organized with UN agencies and other relevant institutions, multiple consultations and policy recommendations have been incorporated in regional and global programmes that address these topics, aiming to create more inclusive and safer homes and cities where every-one can thrive.

The linkages between the environment and the human habitat, including critical issues such as just access to and sustainable use of land, water and food, as well as responsible management and recycling of waste, are also critical part of our concerns. HIC members have been active in developing risk prevention tools, and in rescuing traditional building techniques that recognize the knowledge of the communities and that prioritize the use of local materials. We document and denounce the impacts of climate change faced by the most vulnerable populations and defend the rights of all people affected by disasters to emergency relief and temporary resettlement, the right to remain in their place, and the right to their genuine and effective participation in reconstruction processes.

From its origins, our Coalition has been aware of the relevance of coordinating local and national actions with regional and global presence. Our strategy seeks to strengthen the social actors and processes, while influencing medium and long-term changes through advocacy. This takes many forms including: capacity-building, peer-to-peer exchanges, social mobilization and networking, research collaborations for policy-development, strategic litigation and human rights sensitization of lawyers and judges.

III Challenges and Opportunities Ahead

Denouncing, resisting but also proposing and experimenting are common verbs for organizations affiliated to the Coalition worldwide, and in this path we are not alone. The defence of the territory, the collective management of the commons, the deepening of democracy and the construction of another economy are core concerns and convictions that we share with many voices, who are outraged and concerned about the present and future of life on this planet. HIC has a long history of engagement and active participation in spaces like the World Social Forum, the World Urban

Forum and other international UN agendas, including the Sustainable Development Goals, the Paris Agreement, the Habitat and the New Urban Agenda. The recent publication 'HIC and the Habitat Conferences, 1976-2016' provides reflections from our institutional memory as well as lessons and inspiration for the new generations.

Seeking to effect meaningful and long-lasting change requires great efforts that involve different dimensions and in this regard we must be able to modify our ideas in order to (re)build a (truly) common-sense around these issues and their possible solutions.

From a human rights perspective, housing is much more than four walls and a roof or a property tile. It is then crucial to promote proposals that prioritize the security of tenure, rethinking the importance of public and non-profit rental housing and consolidating cooperatives and other forms of collective or mixed use and ownership. It is also necessary to delineate the substantive differences between the social production of habitat (processes generated by habitable spaces controlled by self-producers, spontaneous or organized, who operate in a not-for-profit manner) and the production of social housing (promoted, build and administrated by public bodies —almost non-existent these days— and/or the private sector).

At the same time, integral housing and habitat policies must be conceived from a territorial scale and take into account the right to the city' strategic principles: the full exercise of citizenship (guaranteeing all human rights for all people in the city, despite their legal status); the social function of land, property and the city (against speculation, evictions and displacement); the democratic management of territory (through direct, participatory and community-oriented democracy); the right to produce the city and a productive habitat (social production and management of habitat); the responsible and sustainable management of the city's commons (including natural and cultural heritage, with an ecological and territorial approach of the city-region and the connection with the rural areas, beyond administrative boundaries); and the equal and democratic enjoyment of the city (access, co-creation and co-management of public spaces, community centres and other such facilities).

The right to the city seeks to create the right to an urban space for solidarity, one that questions agendas that promote the 'competitive' and 'smart' city, which is driven largely by and for corporate interests and political elites. In a context of increasing misogyny, racism, homophobia, and xenophobia, cities are proclaiming themselves to be 'sanctuaries' that welcome migrants and refugees. They 'rebel' in the face of policies that seek to impose austerity and greater social injustice. They denounce the abuses of the big transnational speculative lobbies and they propose ideas like 'human rights cities', 'cities for equity' and 'cities of care', and propose a feminist urbanism and a transversal policy approach that takes into account the material, political and symbolical needs and characteristics of everyday life.

To denounce setbacks, make governments accountable and connect the narratives and practices that are working to build a different world, HIC and its allies, like the *Global Platform for the Right to the City*, are promoting and supporting initiatives such as the *Human Rights Habitat Observatory* or the *International Meeting on Equal Cities* (Buenos Aires, October 2018), as well as the *Municipalist Declaration for the Right to Housing and Right to the City* and *The Shift Campaign*, launched by the UN Special Rapporteur and United Cities and Local Governments (UCLG).

Cities are the concrete places where most of the acute challenges of our times have to be faced and solved. They are also the places of active social mobilization and innovation, indignation and hope.

References and Resources

Committee on Economic, Social and Cultural Rights, *General Comment* No. 4: The Right to Adequate Housing, (New York: United Nations,1991) http://www.refworld.org/pdfid/47a7079a1.pdf

Habitat International Coalition, Habitat International Coalition and the Habitat Conferences 1976-2016, (Barcelona: HIC, 2018), http://hic-gs.org/news.php?pid=7420

International Meeting for Equal Cities, Buenos Aires, 28-31 October 2018, http://hic-gs.org/events-detail.php?pid=7413

Ortiz, E. y L. Zárate, *Vivitos y Coleando. 40 Años Trabajando por el Hábitat Popular en América Latina* [Alive and kicking. 40 years working for people's habitat in Latin America], Mexico City: Universidad Autónoma Metropolitana and HIC-AL, 2002, http://archivo.hic-al.org/publicaciones.cfm?pag=publicpsh

Ortiz, E. y L. Zárate, *De la Marginación a la Ciudadanía. 38 Casos de Producción y Gestión So-cial del Hábitat* [From Marginality to Citizenship. 38 cases of social production and management of habitat], Barcelona: Forum Universal de las Culturas, HIC y HIC-AL, 2004, http://archivo.hic-al.org/publicaciones.cfm?pag=publicpsh

Sassen, S, 'Who Owns our Cities – and Why this Urban Takeover Should Concern us All, *The Guardian*, 24 November 2015, https://www.theguardian.com/cities/2015/nov/24/who-owns-our-cities-and-why-this-urban-takeover-should-concern-us-all

Schechla, Joseph, *Anatomies of a Social Movement. Social Production of Habitat in the Middle East/ North Africa* (Part I), (Cairo: Housing and Land Rights Network-Habitat International Coa-lition, 2004)

Sugranyes, A, and Mathivet C., (eds.), *Cities for All: Proposals and Experiences towards the Right to the City.* (Santiago de Chile: HIC, 2010) http://hic-gs.org/document.php?pid=3848

United Cities and Local Governments, *Municipalist Declaration on the Right to Housing and the Right to the City*, 2018, https://www.uclg.org/sites/default/files/cities_por_adequate_housing.pdf

UN Habitat, *Slum Almanac 2015-2016 - Tracking Improvement in the Lives of Slum Dwellers*, (Nairobi: UN-Habitat, 2016) https://unhabitat.org/slum-almanac-2015-2016/

United Nations, *Sustainable Development Goals*, (New York: United Nations, 2015) https://sustainabledevelopment.un.org/?menu=1300

http://mirror.unhabitat.org/downloads/docs/The_Vancouver_Declaration.pdf

United Nations, UN Special Rapporteur on the Right to Adequate Housing, *Annual Report* February 2017, https://www.ohchr.org/EN/Issues/Housing/Pages/AnnualReports.aspx

United Nations, UN Special Rapporteur on the Right to Adequate Housing, T*he Shift Campaign*, http://www.unhousingrapp.org/the-shift

United Nations, *The Habitat Agenda*, Istanbul: United Nations Conference on Human Settle-ments, June 1996, http://www.un.org/en/events/pastevents/pdfs/habitat_agenda.pdf

United Nations, *The New Urban Agenda*, (Quito: United Nations Conference on Human Settle-ments, October 2016) http://habitat3.org/the-new-urban-agenda/

United Nations, *The Paris Agreement*, (Paris: United Nations Framework Convention on Clima-te Change, 2015), https://unfccc.int/process-and-meetings/the-paris-agreement/the-paris-agreement

United Nations, *The Vancouver Declaration and Action Plan*, (Vancouver: United Nations Con-ference on Human Settlements,1976),

Zárate, Lorena, 'They are Not Informal Settlements – Thy are Habitats Made by People', *The Nature of Cities*, 26 April 2016, https://www.thenatureofcities.com/2016/04/26/they-are-not-informal-settlements-they-are-habitats-made-by-people/

The Third Paradise

MARCO KUSUMAWIJAYA

The future sustainable planet will consist of 'the third Paradises.' They would be neither the original hegemonic nature, the first Paradise that was Eden that were inhabited by innocent Adam and Eve, nor the second Paradise that was the ideal city inhabited by men and God(s) in union, where nothing is natural anymore and everything is transcendental. The third Paradise will be based on a reconstructed relationship between Homo sapiens and nature. It will be a reunited city-region. In each of them will live communities of the third kind which is neither traditional nor modern. They will be communities that are critical to the state, the market and desire.

The future will see Homo sapiens reconciled with nature. Their settlements will be neither urban nor rural, but urban-rural unions. The specific ways of the union will constantly change, but they will be oriented towards making the two more and more in accord with each other. They will keep evolving in unison. Homo sapiens will be knowing and inventing more, increasing their ability to shape the third Paradise.[1] Economy (the norm of the house) will be bent to submit itself to 'ecologics' (the logics of the home).

We will not recreate Eden. With what is left to us --the scorched nature and cracked cities-- we will recover together to a state of common rhythm and accord. More likely, it is Homo sapiens that will submit themselves to nature, and use creativity (a talent unique to Homo sapiens) to develop new attitudes and solutions within its logics.

I Justice
Because of our development outside that logic, we are now faced with not

117

only the challenge of climate change, but also the finiteness of material resource. Justice is an issue of resource distribution. This depends on how a society is organised. Justice is getting ever urgent not only because of the perceived finiteness of resource, but also because of the changes that we need to enact in order to reorganise our society to achieve sustainability, which is not possible without designing it as such as to achieve the long overdue justice at the same time. Without perceived real justice, changes will not motivate all. We can also think of ecological sustainability as giving us yet another, if not the last, chance to achieve justice.

I would like to imagine that communities will be even more important in our future globalized society, because it could encourage critical justice.

By community I mean a group of people who live together in a shared territory, and share some commons in concrete way, with bounds and consequences immediately felt everyday. Size and territorial or spatial limits are essential for the immediate feel of the bounds and consequences. I therefore exclude the modified use of the term community such as in 'community of practice', unless they move towards living together in a bounded space and size. I am neither including those 'imagined communities' and 'institutional communities' such as 'European community', 'ASEAN community', 'International community' and even the 'nation-state'.

As an alternative way of life towards ecological sustainability, community in consequence is a potential a critique towards the state, market and, even more importantly, desire.

Community hence has a progressive critical position to go beyond the treatment of community only as a subject in developmental approach, such as apparent in, among others, phrases like 'community-based development', 'community-driven reconstruction', 'community mapping', etc.

A life in community (defined as in above) can be practiced with the highest consciousness on the imperfection of the state, market and desire, as much as on the imperfection of community itself. It would raise an ambition that community is not a mere a fill-in for the cracks in the nation-state and capitalist system. It is a potential source to produce alternatives (if not substitutes) and, of equal importance, critiques.

As towards desire, a community can play a role not only as a check upon excessive consumption, but also as a source for concepts and practices of sustainable consumption and production, at least to prevent us from falling into 'tragedy of the commons'. Community is an functional ideology to produce more *commons* and a worthy place in itself to locate more commons. Community could be a source to produce new relations in living together, in a system of collaborative consumption and production, and in giving meanings to, or making sense out of, co-existence with 'others.'

What needs to be emphasised more is that community can be a critique towards desire.

We do not yet know for sure how the struggle with climate change and finite resource will eventually play out. There are some scenarios. I would argue, though, that how we criticize our desire will change the game.

Somehow we have now a consensus that there is a need for an ecological transition that must have been initiated earlier. Ecological transition is a process whereby we change our living system to be within the system of the earth and its principles in line with the logics of the house, the earth.

Changes at individual level is never sufficient. Changes need to be tested out, rooted at the level of 'living together', the locus where more complex but unavoidable relationships take place. An ecologically sustainable mode of living together must be discovered or constructed in a viable scale and level of community.

Within ecological perspective, consumption is at the very core of desire. Related to it are deeper and sometimes hidden layers: ambition for universal prosperity, power, industrial complex and vested interest, expansion of living space into nature and others' territories and so on.

Communities, through a process of dialogue and open communication, could provide bounds and is a moderating voice. It may begin with posing questions to distinguish needs from wants, and moves towards exploring alternatives that might or might not be limiting or offering new abundance. 'Is there a sustainable consumption and production?' This is the question that should lead to invention of new economy and forms of state as they are constructed to cater to our desire. Thinking about them cannot be fundamental enough without thinking about our desire. Community can be a meaningful critique of consumption and production when it also discusses desire.

II Is city a community?

In South East Asia in the course of between the 15th and 17th centuries urbanity started identically with modernity. So were urban communities. It changed the perception of the world, oneself, and time and space. Two

119

centuries later cities in South East Asia had served as a source of critique towards colonial states. It should be a critique of contemporary forms of state as well. A city, being the most sophisticated form of living together in the most intense and dense conditions, provides many commons, including goods and narratives. But there are current, continuous and persistent threats to itself being a common. It is therefore also urgent that the city, for it to remain a community, to also critique itself. The city in its long history has been changing individuals and civilisations. It can be changed fundamentally, too, in the way it uses energy and materials.

So, yes, a city can be a community, one that is more real than a nation state, as long as it is productive in creating and maintaining commons, being critical to itself and others. Most encroachment and transformation of commons into public (state-owned) and private properties take place increasingly and intensely mostly in the process of urbanisation.

III Optimism
Actually the vision above should not look like being too far away. There have been already emerging thoughts, theories, sciences, techniques and practices that are creating new paths of reconnecting with nature. A quick browse reveals Deep Ecology[2] at philosophical level. In economics there have been environmental, green and ecological economics. At production level there are Blue Economy[3] and circular economy based on the science of circular metabolism. There are many emerging ecological recovery practices such as (re-)naturalization of streams, organic and circular farming. In city making there is water sensitive approach. Many things are labelled 'green' nowadays: Green Building, Green Energy, Green Materials, etc. Although we have to be cautious of 'green-washing', the green labelling indicates some good wills and imperfect thoughts that include in themselves opportunity for improvements.

In some cities the politics of solidarity is in circulation again to reconstruct urban communities. Artists have for sometime been working with communities to build some kind of new consciousness together towards co-production of commons.

Vis-à-vis the state whose power is based on hegemonic rationality there are at the other end indigenous communities that are still living with their own norms. Many marine and forest conservation programs in Indonesia are based on and use rules available and effective in local communities. The reconstruction of Aceh after the 2004 tsunami involved many autonomous initiatives by local communities. Efforts are being made to see how the multiple logics contained in these norms, principles, rules and practices can transcend their contextual limits and brought into the future.

Notes

1. A concept I borrow from a talk by Italian artist Michelangelo Pistoletto given in Berlin in 2011; cfr. Michelangelo Pistoletto, Il terzo Paradiso, Marsilio, Venezia 2010.
2. Hicham-Stéphane Afeissa, articles « Deep ecology/Écologie profonde » et « Næss, Arne (1912-2009) » in Dominique Bourg et Alain Papaux, Dictionnaire de la pensée écologique, Presses universitaires de France, 2015.
3. Cfr. https://www.gunterpauli.com/the-blue-economy.html.

The Periphery in the Centre

LUIZ KOHARA

The population living in the peripheral regions of the city of São Paulo, the richest city in the country, suffer from the economic, social, and geographical inequalities of the city, penalized by the lack of adequate public services of education, health care, welfare, leisure, culture, and public transportation, living in a condition of exile in the city itself. Poor families seek to live in the central areas, where there is better urban infrastructure and alternatives for work, but they find extremely precarious housing in the slums at very high cost. Since 1988, the Gaspar Garcia Centre for Human Rights has struggled for the rights of this excluded population and has been able to improve living conditions for marginalized families by guaranteeing the right to own housing and through social insertion.

The city of São Paulo, the richest in the country, is a clear expression of the contradictions generated by economic, social, and geographical inequalities, setting up extremely contrasting realities in urban spaces. On the one hand, there are regions or "centres" with urban infrastructure, public services, availability of cultural activities, and environmental quality, on the other hand are the "peripheries," distant from areas with greater availability of work, without adequate public services of education, health care, welfare, leisure, culture, and public transportation, with a precarious infrastructure of basic sanitation and drinkable water.

The population of the city of São Paulo spends, on average, 2.42 hours per day commuting between home and work. However, for the large proportion of those living in the more distant peripheries, this time exceeds four hours per day, which means sacrificing school development, family life, leisure, and time for other needs. In addition, there is a high

123

cost for commuting. Thus, due to the difficulties of urban mobility, the poorer peripheral populations live in exile in the city itself.

For the poor population, living in distant peripheries without adequate infrastructure, also means a greater risk of being victims of violence. Numerous studies show that the regions that concentrate violence are those where there is no presence of the state to meet the basic needs of the population. The segregated and fragile areas in which young people have a low opportunity for social insertion have been occupied by criminal organizations, which in many cases have indiscriminate relationships with public security agents, causing residents to live in insecure conditions. In 2016, more than 62,000 homicides occurred in Brazilian cities (IPEA, 2018, p. 93), affecting, for the most part, Afro-descendant youth living in segregated and poverty-concentrated areas.

In the city of São Paulo, the chance of a resident of a peripheral neighbourhood with a concentration of poverty being murdered is 43.3 times more than a resident of a neighbourhood where the population with a high purchasing power is concentrated. This same comparison exists between neighbourhoods in relation to life expectancy; there is a difference of 23.7 years, respectively: 55.7 years and 79.4 years.[2] These inequalities reverberate in family economic differences and public services available in the neighbourhoods. Among the 31 sub-prefectures,[3] the seven located in the central region of the city have 2/3 of the hospital beds and 2/3 of the formal jobs available in the city.

Urban sprawl, in the interests of the real estate sector, has expended a large share of public resources for areas already valued or that will become valued, to the detriment of the social needs of the poorest populations, as well as favouring concentration of land ownership and urban inequality. In the city of São Paulo, 1% of the owners (22,400 people) account for 25% of all properties registered in the city, which represents 45% of the municipal real estate value.[4]

Inequality in the city is also expressed in relation to environmental quality. Low-income families, as they cannot access housing in the formal market, build their homes in areas with geological hazards, flooding during periods of rain, areas at the edge of streams or contaminated areas. These are areas without public investment in sewage sanitation, afforestation, and squares, with very low environmental quality.

I The struggle of the poor in the centre of the city

In São Paulo, low-income families are always trying to live in the central areas of the city for ease of transport, greater availability of formal and informal jobs, and the presence of public social services, like hospitals, schools, daycare, welfare. However, the housing alternatives found by low-income workers in the centre are tenements.[5]

The history of the city centre of São Paulo is marked by disputes between the interests of enrichment and the presence of the poor in tenements. The centre- a privileged place for public investment, concentrating the main institutions of economic, political, and religious power, as well as the housing and cultural spaces of the wealthy class- cannot be the place of housing for and coexistence with the popular class. With this understanding, the public powers, from time to time, have launched projects of revitalization or restoration of the centre with the objectives of hygiene and social gentrification.

Even so, large numbers of low-income families live in the centre, because of the economic interests of those who rent out the housing in the tenements due to their high profitability; however, to continue living in the centre they remain hostages to exploitation. The value of the lease of a room, of about 10 m², in a tenement located in the central region of the city,[6] is about R$ 800, while the minimum wage is R$ 954.[7] Due to this situation, the tenants say "if you eat, you do not live, if you live, you do not eat."

Faced with the contradiction between the needs of the poor population and the presence of hundreds of abandoned buildings in the centre, which do not fulfil a social function according to the Federal Constitution, a large number of families have occupied these properties in the central area in recent years. In addition, in the centre, there are thousands of individuals and families living on the streets, sidewalks, squares, marquises, under viaducts and other places, without any adequate physical protection or privacy, constituting the most dramatic expression of social vulnerability, violence, and human cruelty. The population on the street seeks out this region for the possibility of informal services and survival.

The centre also is disputed by informal workers who survive on street commerce, in its near totality, illegal, because the Prefecture does not recognize this activity in the valued areas of the city. Part of the workers' routine is persecution and harassment by public agents.

In the centre of the city of São Paulo is the presence of what could be called a social periphery.

II The performance of the Gaspar Garcia Centre for Human Rights (CGGDH) in relation to the periphery in the centre

The CGGDH was founded in 1988 with the mission of struggling for the human rights of the poor, who lived in the slums or slept on the streets as well as those who worked as collectors of recyclables or street vendors, to gain the right to live and work with dignity in the centre of the city. Currently, their operation is across the entire city of São Paulo among differing social realities.

The actions of CGGDH have always been directed toward the populations that are victims of social exclusion, to organize collectives, such as housing, homelessness, and material collectors' movements, street vendors' forums, and associations for the struggle for rights, to influence public policies and search for alternatives to improve living conditions.

In this action to achieve rights, with the strengthening of population organizations, there are important advances, among which the following stand out: municipal, state, and federal governments have implemented social interest housing programs in the city centre, serving, in the last 20 years, more than five thousand families who lived in the tenements and slums, thousands of families through legal defence and influence in public institutions, guaranteeing the right to own housing; hundreds of people on the street achieved social insertion, leaving the street; co-operatives of individual collectors of reusable materials were constituted, which brought improvements in the income of the co-operative members; implementation of public social policies for the homeless population, allowing greater social integration; workers and street vendors started to struggle for the right to decent work in a collective way, ensuring better working conditions; police violence against the poorest has been confronted; contributions were made in urban development policies toward social inclusion and environmental sustainability.

There is an immense periphery of poverty in the centre of the city. The challenges are many! All the advances obtained had participation by the population itself and many experiences of mutual solidarity. Improvements in housing and work conditions have made it possible for the children of the beneficiaries, for example, to access universities and families to live with dignity. The achievements that Gaspar Garcia has been making show

126

that it is possible for the poor to live with dignity in the centre.
This walk alongside the periphery in the centre of the city is animated by faith and hope for a more just and fraternal world.

Translated by Thia Cooper

Bibliography

IBGE. Instituto Brasileiro de Geografia e Estatística. Síntese de Indicadores Sociais 2017. *Caderno Estudos & Pesquisas*: informação demográfica e socioeconômica – 37. Available at: <https://biblioteca.ibge.gov.br/visualizacao/livros/liv101459.pdf>. Accessed: 19 August, 2018.

IPEA; FBSP. Instituto de Pesquisa Econômica Aplicada; Fórum Brasileiro de Segurança Pública. *Atlas da Violência* 2018. Brasília: IPEA (2018).

OXFAM. *Relatório A distância que nos une: um retrato das desigualdades brasileiras*. OXFAM Brasil (2017). Available at: <www.oxfam.org.br>. Accessed: 20 July, 2018.

REDE NOSSA SÃO PAULO. Blog. 2 August, 2016. Available at: <https://www.nossasaopaulo.org.br/noticias/nossa-sao-paulo-apresenta-balanco-do-plano-de-metas-e-mapa-da-desigualdade-atualizado>. Accessed: 19 August, 2018.

_____. *Mapa da desigualdade* 2017. São Paulo (2017). Available at: <www.nossasaopaulo.org.br>. Accessed: 10 July, 2018.

The Death Penalty, Church Teaching and the Development of Dogma: Reflections on Pope Francis' Change to the Catechism

MICHAEL SEEWALD

Starting from the change to the Catechism, which makes the death penalty inadmissible from now on from the perspective of moral theology, the article offers a systematic analysis of relationship of the Catholic Church to the death penalty. It first outlines the complex ways in which the problem of the death penalty has been handled in the various Christian traditions. The focus then switches to the argument used by Pope Francis, that the death penalty contradicts the 'dignity of the person', and finally there is a discussion of how far the Pope's decision forms a seamless part of the Church's teaching office as commonly understood or is a break with it

I Introduction

As Cardinal Luis F. Ladaria announced on 1 August 2018 in a letter to bishops, Pope Francis has modified the *Catechism of the Catholic Church*. Whereas the *Catechism* previously taught that 'legitimate public authority has the right and duty to inflict penalties commensurate with the gravity of the crime... The traditional teaching of the Church does not exclude... recourse to the death penalty (*Catechism*, 2266-2267), we are now told that 'The death penalty is inadmissible because it is an attack on the inviolability and dignity of the person,' and the Church 'therefore works with determination for its abolition worldwide' (Catechism, 2267, new version).

A group of predominantly US academics, priests and journalists regards this teaching as wrong and therefore addressed an appeal to the College of Cardinals via the magazine First Things.[1] The cardinals, the appeal says, have a duty, 'before God and before the Church', to persuade the Pope to 'withdraw' the change to the Catechism in order once more 'to teach the word of God unadulterated'. The reasons that should have a 'seriously binding' effect on the consciences of the cardinals are weighty. A ban on capital punishment contradicts holy scripture:

'Whoever sheds the blood of a human,
by a human shall that person's blood be shed;
for in his own image
God made humankind' (Gen 9.6).

This and, in the view of the petitioners, 'many other biblical texts' show that the death penalty is not intrinsically evil, because it has been authorised, and sometimes even ordered, by God. 'The Church holds that Scripture cannot teach moral error. The legitimacy in principle of capital punishment is also the consistent teaching of the magisterium for two millennia. To contradict scripture and tradition on this point would cast doubt on the credibility of the magisterium in general,' argue the signatories, who say they wish to draw attention to the 'gravely scandalous situation' into which the Pope has brought the Church. The cardinals are reminded that it is 'a truth contained in the Word of God, and taught by the ordinary and universal magisterium of the Catholic Church,' that 'criminals may lawfully be put to death by the civil power'. By 'refusing to teach this doctrine', the Pope, they say, has 'brought confusion upon the Church' and given rise to the impression 'that the Church considers, contrary to the Word of God, that capital punishment is intrinsically evil'. The cardinals, say the writers, should 'advise the Pope that it is his duty to put an end to this scandal, to withdraw this paragraph from the Catechism, and to teach the word of God unadulterated'.

The best answer to the sort of fundamentalism displayed in appeal published by *First Things* is not indignation, but what fundamentalists fear most, distinction. For example, one question might be: Have the signatories of the appeal realised how controversial the interpretation of the text they cite as a *locus classicus* (Gen 9.6) in fact is, and that it seems doubtful that this passage can be adduced at all to justify the death penalty?[2] The signatories point to a biblical text that allegedly has

God himself advocating the death penalty and claim that it should be followed because scripture contains no moral errors. So what do they do about the Old Testament legal texts that generously stipulate the death penalty for all manner of offences? So, according to Leviticus, two men who have sexual relations with each other are to be punished by death (Lev 20.13). Is that also God's inerrant word, to be put into effect? Today when homosexuals are executed, would the Church have no objection to make because that has been decreed by God's morally infallible word? If theologians are no longer able to see scripture and tradition as what they are, that is 'human interpretations',[3] that always need interpretation and require critical analysis, we are on the edge of an abyss in civilisation that in the name of divine progress points us to the rule of force.

The rest of this article will focus on two points of the appeal of those who believe that the Church is violating its divine mandate if it denies the death penalty theological legitimacy: the claim that the legitimacy of the death penalty has been a constant doctrine of 'the ordinary and universal magisterium' of the Church, and the thesis that the alteration of the catechism casts 'doubt on the credibility of the magisterium in general'.

II The Catholic Church and the death penalty: some historical snapshots

The Church has had to grapple with the issue of the death penalty in two related but distinct contexts, in defining its relationship to civil authority and in considering the question whether people classed as heretics should be punished with the death penalty.[4]

2.1 The Church position on the death penalty as a matter of state law

The New Testament says nothing about the legitimacy or illegitimacy of the death penalty as a matter of state policy, but it has Jesus going to his death as an innocent man condemned by the competent authority as a criminal, which illustrates that even an authority assumed to have received power 'from above' (Jn 19.11) can misuse that power and reach wrong judgments. In other words, Christianity confesses as redeemer someone whom himself was the victim of the death penalty, a fate which many of the first disciples shared, such as Stephen (Acts 7.57-60), a victim of religiously inspired mob violence, or Paul (1 Clement 5.6-7), as a condemned Roman citizen. For the Church fathers, just as important as the fact that founding figures of Christianity were forced to suffer the death penalty seems to have been the fact that these victims did not oppose this fate. According to a saying attributed to Jesus, those who sought to do one harm were not to be resisted (Mt 5.39), and according to Paul's teaching, the governing authorities, who bear the sword and are servants of God, are to be obeyed (Rom 13.16).

Because the death penalty was part of the range of penalties regarded as legitimate in the Roman empire, the Church fathers saw no fundamental incompatibility between their faith and the imposition of the death penalty. This made it possible to adopt contemporary theories of punishment. Clement of Alexandria, for example, accepted the Platonic idea of the twofold purpose of punishment. Punishment served, according to Plato's *Gorgias*, either to improve a person or to be a deterrent example.[5] Those who could still be led to a reformed life should be given the precise measure of suffering they need to improve, but those who are 'incurable' (*aniatos*) should be killed because they themselves can no longer gain any benefit from punishment aimed at improvement and through their death society in general would gain moral benefit at least in the form of deterrence. This argument was taken up by Clement of Alexandria and used in the popular Christian metaphor of the body: If a limb of the body was incurably (*aniatos*) diseased, it had to be amputated for the sake of the health of the body as a whole.[6] Clement, however, did not adopt Plato's critical political point, that the worst of the incurables were to be found among the tyrants, kings and rulers,[7] that is those who had made most use of the death penalty against others.

Irrespective of the right of the secular power to impose death penalties, there was nevertheless a conviction in Christianity that it was more moral not to carry out such sentences. According to Ambrose of Milan, what authority decides is one thing, what compassion suggests, another. Anyone who carries out a legitimately imposed death sentence bears no guilt, but the person who does not carry it out deserves praise.[8] This attitude reflects the practice that bishops from the 4th century onwards often interceded for those condemned to death to prevent the implementation of the sentence. And where they themselves in late antiquity – like Augustine, for example – exercised judicial functions, they did not impose this sentence, but tried to give offenders the possibility of repentance in this life instead of bringing them directly before God's judgment seat bearing the burden of their sins.[9] The Christian attitude was thus ambivalent: on the one hand it was recognised that the state had the right to impose the death penalty, but there was also the tendency to prevent its implementation and to exercise a moderating effect on the state. This ambiguity also runs through the middle ages and continues into the 19th century. After the early middles ages, in which – surprising as this may be to readers today with their cliché-ridden view of this period – the death penalty was rarely and reluctantly imposed,[10] as Christian scepticism about the death penalty and pastoral insistence on repentance in this life possibly bore fruit, the idea of the death penalty came back into vogue, as the idea of the 'peace of God' shows, as part of pacification programmes. 'After centuries in which the normative texts had given priority to catalogues of penances, we now appear to have again for the first time a penal authority with the confidence to impose these harsh penalties While the idea of the death penalty and the penal justice of rulers had never been completely forgotten, it was only in rare cases, such as attacks on kings and potentates of the kingdom, that rulers dared to display their power so clearly.'[11] So Pope Innocent III – according to a 1210 addition to a letter of 1208 – taught that the secular power (*potestas secularis*) 'may without mortal sin carry out a capital sentence provided that it takes the step of executing the sentence not from hatred, but by virtue of a judicial decision, not without prudence but after reflection' (Denzinger-Hünermann, 795). Where bishops – for example, in the Holy Roman Empire – were themselves secular rulers, they also had the right to apply secular justice, which could include the death penalty. Consequently, from the high middle ages onwards death sentences were passed and carried out in the name of bishops, though in their role as territorial rulers. The same was true of the Pope and his ecclesiastical territory until its dissolution.[12] Nonetheless in the spiritual context the awareness that the death penalty was a problematic means of producing justice never disappeared. One illustration of this is that clerics were given *privilegium fori*, which meant that their affairs were dealt with, not before a secular court, but by an ecclesiastical one, which could not impose the death penalty. And the continuing reservations about the death penalty led to a situation in which religious bodies such as monasteries took in refugees who were liable to the death penalty if caught, and granted them asylum. As a result, in the inherited territories of the Hapsburg empire in the reign of Maria Theresia, clerics were threatened with punishment as 'violators of the supreme decrees' if they took in deserters and surrendered them only on condition that the state would declare that the death penalty would not be applied.[13]

2.2 The death penalty for Christian heretics

Those who, like the writers of the appeal against the change to the catechism, think that the theological legitimacy of the death penalty is based on the fact that it is 'a truth contained in the Word of God', and cite the Old Testament, ignore, first, the different ways this topic is dealt with in the Old Testament, and, second, that the New Testament intervenes in this debate to provide a corrective. For the early Christians there was a fundamental difference between what is due to God and what is due to the emperor (Mt 22.21). They distinguished the social rules within their community from the civil power, which Paul describes as *exousia* (Rom 13.1). The Old Testament legal texts, in which God is shown as lawgiver for both the political and the worshipping community of Israel (e.g. Ex 19-40), who therefore both regulates what in Pauline terms is the sphere of the civil *exousia* and sets the norms for religious life, are unfamiliar with this New Testament distinction. Instead they maintain the ideal of civil and religious unity and are prepared to punish violations of the integrity of this unity, if necessary, by death. Jesus and the early Christians saw things differently.[14]

Whereas in the book of Leviticus blasphemers and enemies of God are to be killed (Lev 24.16), the New Testament rules out such a course, although its authors were familiar with the fact of enmity with God and blasphemy. Paul talks about 'enemies of the cross of Christ' (Phil 3.18), and the Letter of James accuses adulterers of cultivating friendship with the world and thus incurring 'enmity with God' (Jas 4.4). The key correction to Old Testament legal provisions, however, consists in the fact that these religious situations were no longer punished by death. On the contrary, Jesus tells his disciples, 'Love your enemies' (Mt 5.44). Now, when blasphemous behaviour provoked a reaction from the community, this did not consist in the use of violence, but in social sanctions. In a case of a sexual offence, in which a man had slept with his father's wife, where the book of Leviticus calls for the death penalty (Lev 20.11), Paul orders that the man (!) involved should be expelled from the community and handed over 'to Satan' for 'the destruction of his flesh, so that his spirit may be saved on the day of the Lord' (1 Cor 5.1-5). There is no mention of punishment by death, as the Old Testament calls for in such a case, or any other physical punishment. The ultimate judgment about the life and death, salvation and damnation of the blasphemer is left to God. Rainer Forst comments: 'This is a central point in Christian ideas of tolerance: on earth no human being should venture to pass a judgment that belongs to God alone – it is his justice that will carry out the punishment.'[15] Accordingly, the early Christian community refrained from the physical punishment, still less killing, of blasphemers or false teachers.

This began to change in the 4th century through the increasingly close amalgamation of the religious rules of the Church and the civil order of the empire. The 'duty of an emperor, which had "grown up" over centuries, to ensure the *pax deorum* by establishing and preserving unity of worship,'[16] was transferred to the role the emperors (except Julian the Apostate) assumed in the Church. They saw themselves as the guarantors of unity, demonstrated first by Constantine's intervention in the Arian controversy, in the turning of dogmatic decisions into imperial decrees with legal force and their enforcement, by exile if necessary. Towards the end of the 4th century this intervention increased to the point of the application of physical force. The first killing of a heretic took place in 385 at the imperial palace in Trier, where Priscillian, a condemned heretic from Iberia, was executed. For many bishops – including those who rejected Priscillian's teaching, such as Martin of Tours and Ambrose of Milan – this execution was a 'scandal, because an internal Church matter, essentially of dogmatic theology, was being decided by the emperor's secular court with the shedding of blood'.[17] As a result Martin, Ambrose, and also Siricius, the bishop of Rome, broke off communion with the bishops who had taken part in Priscillian's trial. The protest had its effect: in this period there is no report of any other execution of a heretic, and in the eastern Roman empire down to the fall of Constantinople there was not a single case of the execution of a person condemned as a heretic for his religious beliefs.[18]

The Latin West, however, took a different course in the middle ages. Over time the view that prevailed was not that of Ambrose or Martin, but that of their younger contemporary Augustine, who produced a typological interpretation of the *compelle intrare* ('Compel them to come in') from Luke's parable of the great dinner (Lk 14.23) according to which the civil power had an auxiliary role in the creation of Christian orthodoxy and Church unity, which included measures of physical force against heretics.[19] So-called political Augustinianism, as it developed from late antiquity, on the one hand assigned the state a subordinate function in relation to the spiritual power, but on the other gave it – insofar as it was prepared to serve the spiritual realm, a sacral legitimation.[20] While it was the role of the Church to determine the orthodoxy or heterodoxy of a person, those it regarded as heretics it transferred to the civil power, which used the legal measures at its command, which from the high middle ages onwards included, with increasing frequency, the death penalty, to punish heresies by execution. The IV Lateran Council even confirmed this division of responsibility as doctrine. Condemned heretics were transferred to the 'secular powers or their administrators' (COD II, 233), who ensured that an ecclesiastical judgment concerned with dogmatic matters led to the imposition of a secular punishment. In this way heresy was transferred to the sphere of secular law, where it counted as *lèse-majesté* against a ruler who based his legitimacy on the sacred, and who punished it correspondingly harshly, even by death.[21]

2.3 The legitimacy of the death penalty, constant teaching of the Church

The appeal to the cardinals claims: 'The legitimacy in principle of capital punishment is… the consistent teaching of the magisterium for two millennia.' After the points made above this thesis ought to seem questionable. Quite apart from the fact that the idea of an 'ordinary magisterium', which the appeal cites in support of its position, has not existed for two thousand years, but only since 1863, when it was cited for the first time ever, by Pius IX (Denzinger-Hünermann, 2879), a look at the positions taken by the Church on the death penalty shows a complex situation. Whereas the early Christian communities refrained from any form of physical punishment – even where Old Testament regulations prescribe it – they accepted the right of the civil authority to impose a legal system that Christians were obliged to obey. At the same time there were signs of discomfort with the death penalty, illustrated by pressure from bishops for it not to be carried out and for the offender instead to be given earthly penances. If this ideal was partially achieved in the early middle ages, from the high middle ages onwards there was a shift in favour of the death penalty, which the Church recognised as legal provided it was based on a 'well-considered' (Denzinger-Hünermann, 795) judicial sentence. In addition the Church indirectly participated in executions by the state when it surrendered to the secular power people it considered to be heretics. Nonetheless, discomfort within the Church never completely disappeared, as shown by the constant interventions of clerics to protect those condemned from the application of the sentence. It is therefore impossible to claim a consistent position, maintained for two millennia, in favour of the death penalty.

III The Pope's decision: the dignity of the person

The historical data summarised here should not be misused for apologetic purposes. Its purpose is merely to show that history is not as unequivocal as the fundamentalists fighting for the death penalty would like it to be. Nevertheless it is true that the Church in its dealings with the death penalty has incurred great guilt. This is especially true of the heresy trials, in which clerics, aware that they were acting in the name of divine truth, gave people up to death and at the same time were able to maintain the illusion that they were keeping their hands clean. This is a blot on the Church's history, and should be remembered as such. A culture of remembrance that preserves not only the memory of the misdeeds and violence of others, such as were inflicted on Christian martyrs and confessors, but also remembers its own misdeeds and violence as a warning to itself, has hitherto had little currency in the Church. The Church's elephant- like memory that commemorates injustice suffered by the Church stands in contrast to the almost pathological failure of memory that allows injustice carried out by the Church, even in quite recent times, to be forgotten all too quickly. But both dimensions of memory are important. The Church honours her martyrs and confessors because they show what great things faith is capable of. But the Church should not only keep the memory of her role as victim, but also of the times she was the aggressor, so that she does not forget what shameful acts faith is capable of. Recognising this ambivalence is part of the honesty without which religion becomes ideology.

It is also honest to remain open for a growth of knowledge, even when this additional knowledge leads to self-examination. Since from the 18th century, beginning with the writings of Cesare Beccaria, criticism of the death penalty became louder, more and more governments, especially in the 20th century, have abolished the death penalty, especially in Europe, though not exclusively. The US state of Michigan, for example, in 1864 was one of the first states to delete the death penalty from its laws. While the arguments against the death penalty are many and varied, one is frequently mentioned, the idea of an inalienable dignity, which belongs even to those who have not respected the dignity of others. The Church, however, has no right to quickly pocket this idea and claim it for itself. Christian talk of *dignitas* often referred, not to a quality that made all people equal, such as is expressed in the concept of human dignity, but a special value attaching to Christians.[22] Nevertheless there was also a recognition in the Church, even beyond religious differences, of areas of intimate individuality belonging to every human being that demanded – from that person and others – absolute respect. Thomas Aquinas gives the example of conscience,[23] though that still did not make Thomas an opponent of the death penalty. Hans Joas argues the view that these ideas from Christian thought gradually came to stand on their own and influenced the idea of just punishments. The characteristic feature of this process, which Joas, drawing on Émile Durkheim, describes as the 'consecration of the person', and in which he sees 'a development of Judaeo-Christian ideas',[24] shows itself, he says, in the fact that the 'same aura is attributed to the person' as that 'inherent in holy things'.[25] For the assessment of crime and punishment, Joas says, this had ambivalent effects: on the one hand, the idea of the sacredness of every person led to the rejection of torture and the death penalty, but on the other crimes seemed all the more deserving of punishment the more they violated the sacredness of every person, so that a tension appeared 'between the need to punish every violation of the sacredness of the person and the same violation of that sacredness inherent in the act of punishment'.[26] When people hear of a dreadful crime, moral indignation and outrage grow the more the life of a person is held sacred. At the same time there is still the moral demand on oneself not to repay the offender in kind and so not to destroy the sacredness of someone who has violated the sacredness of another person, despite the desire to punish them.

Pope Francis recognises this development as a legitimate part of Catholic tradition, even though – despite Joas' attempt to co-opt it for an apologetic on behalf of the institutional Church – it took place for the most part outside the Church's institutional structures, while of course working with Christian ideas: 'Recourse to the death penalty on the part of legitimate authority, following a fair trial, was long considered an appropriate response to the gravity of certain crimes and an acceptable, albeit extreme, means of safeguarding the common good. Today, however, there is an increasing awareness that the dignity of the person is not lost even after the commission of very serious crimes' (*Catechism*, 2267, revised version). It is therefore the inalienable dignity of the person that rules out killing even someone who has taken a life. Moreover, Francis contrasts his view with the old version of the catechism when he says: 'A new understanding has emerged of the significance of penal sanctions imposed by the state' (*Catechism*, 2267, revised version). The 1992 version had still read: 'The primary purpose of the penalty is to redress the disorder caused by the offence' (*Catechism*, 2266, adapted). Neither the protection of the public nor the rehabilitation of the offender are given priority here, but the idea of a quasi-metaphysical order disrupted by the crime that has to be restored by the punishment. Francis, in contrast, stresses that punishment for a crime that has been committed serves only two purposes, the security of the public and the rehabilitation of the offender. To achieve the first, the death penalty, he says, is not necessary, because 'more effective systems of detention have been developed, which ensure the due protection of citizens,' and it is detrimental to the second because it 'definitively [deprives] the guilty of the possibility of redemption' (*Catechism*, 2267, revised version).

IV The crisis of attempts to enhance the continuity of the magisterium

The signatories of the appeal claim that the Pope's decision 'would cast doubt on the credibility of the magisterium in general', because they believe they have found it to be a breach with scripture and tradition. As I have argued, on a more nuanced examination scripture and tradition are not as unequivocal as the signatories suggest. Nevertheless, they are right in the sense that the magisterium of the Catholic Church has never before so unequivocally spoken against the legitimacy of the death penalty and argued for its abolition as a matter of principle. Here Pope Francis has introduced something new. It is precisely here that there is a problem for theologians who regard themselves as the authority that confirms the latest decisions of the magisterium: something new that definitely does not behave as though it is in seamless agreement with the old teaching cannot exist, if we are to judge by the architecture adopted by the magisterium in the 19th century, which continues until today – although Pope Francis is taking a different course. The magisterium has got itself trapped in an ideology of continuity.

The problem is that it sees itself as having the following *mandate*: 'It is this Magisterium's task to preserve God's people from deviations and defections and to guarantee them the objective possibility of professing the true faith without error' (*Catechism*, 890). Christians are evidently constantly exposed to confusions that the cannot withstand with the resources of their own reason and the power of their faith. They are t herefore dependent on the wise guidance of the magisterium, which preserves 'the true faith without error' and so offers all those who willingly follow it the 'objective' possibility of believing what is correct. The magisterium can do this by virtue of a specific gift: the idea of supernatural assistance, reserved to the bishops and the Pope, that is often associated with the holy Spirit. The magisterium derives its activity from a mission and a gift: it serves the Word of God, 'teaching only what has been handed on, listening to it devoutly, guarding it scrupulously and explaining it faithfully in accord with a divine commission and with the help of the Holy Spirit, it draws from this one deposit of faith everything which it presents for belief as divinely revealed' (Vatican II, *Dei Verbum* 10). This creates an obligation for all the faithful that is described in the *Catechism* as a statement of fact that has the force of a command: 'Mindful of Christ's words to his apostles: "He who hears you, hears me," the faithful receive with docility the teachings and directives that their pastors give them in different forms' (*Catechism*, 87). In this sort of ideologically watertight legitimation narrative there is no provision for explicit second thoughts, and therefore doctrinal innovations, which do take place in the Church, especially when it is claimed that what is being taught is the tradition and what was always the teaching, have to be disguised under the appearance of continuity. Theological innovation therefore usually takes place with the innovation disguised. The magisterium has established two strategies for dealing with this. Either it is denied that a new idea is new, and it is suggested that what has been taught now is what has always been taught, or a position that is no longer tenable is quietly dropped and it is hoped that no-one will notice. An example of the first strategy is advocacy for freedom of religion and conscience, which has only been part of the Church's teaching since the Second Vatican Council (Denzinger-Hünermann, 4240). The Church's own failure, the fact that until Vatican II the Church made every effort to suppress what at the Council it recognised as a right of the human person, is nowhere addressed. The fact that Popes Gregory XVI and Pius IX described freedom of religion and conscience as sheer 'madness',27 and so condemned it (DH 2915), is not mentioned in the conciliar text or in any of the preparatory or subsequent texts on the matter. Similarly, the break that Vatican II's *Dignitatis Humanae* represents with the magisterium's pronouncements from the end of the 18th to the middle of the 20th centuries is never discussed.[28]

An example of the second model of doctrinal development – letting a teaching quietly expire – is the Church's position that all human beings are descended from Adam and Eve, so-called monogenism. As late as 1950, Pope Pius XII had taught that the theory of evolution could only be applied to human beings if it could still be maintained that all human beings descend biologically from a single set of parents, the couple Adam and Eve, thought to be historical figures (DH 3897). This view of the ordinary magisterium was subsequently no longer followed and does not appear at all in the 1992 edition of the *Catechism of the Catholic Church*. This would have given it crucial importance in the architecture of the Church's magisterium. It is a doctrine from the so-called secondary field, which was regarded as necessary to support what was regarded as a revealed article of faith, the doctrine of original sin. The magisterium allowed Pius XII's statement to disappear quietly, never officially corrected it, because in terms of its own logic it simply cannot do so without risking the collapse of this house of cards of its own making. Accordingly, this embarrassing teaching of Pius XII's is instead discreetly ignored, to leave the magisterium, and the people who are supposed to be given 'the objective possibility of professing the true faith without error' (*Catechism*, 890), with the illusion of infallible continuity. The fact that time has been called on this game from the top of the Church, and a Pope has the confidence, quite openly, without any presentational cover-up, to contrast what was taught 'for a long time' with what should be taught 'today' provokes anger in some Church circles, and this anger becomes ever more extreme and loses the gift of making distinctions. There were dogmatic innovations in past pontificates too, but they couldn't be called that. That has now changed.

IV Looking to the future

It is hard to avoid the impression that the criticism of the Pope's position on the death penalty is simply an expression of the dissatisfaction of a minority of theologians with the style of the Pope's teaching in general. With the withdrawal of Church legitimation for the practice of the death penalty, however, the 'long time' and 'today' came so visibly into conflict that this decision became a touchstone. It is to be hoped that in both questions – his style of teaching in general and his teaching on the death penalty in particular – the Pope will not be shaken. Church authority is not a means of theological self-assertion. That was something many theologians in ear-

Michael Seewald

lier pontificates had to learn painfully, and which other theologians, who
so far seem to have been spared that experience, still have to learn under
Pope Francis.

Translated by Francis McDonagh

Notes

1. See 'An Appeal to the Cardinals of the Catholic Church (15.08.2018)', in: https://
www.firstthings.com/web-exclusives/2018/08/an-appeal-to-the-cardinals-of-the-catholic-
church, accessed 12.01.2019. The quotations that follow are taken from this text.
2. See Johannes Schnocks, *Das Alte Testament und die Gewalt. Studien zu göttlicher und
menschlicher Gewalt in alttestamentlichen Texten und ihren Rezeptionen*, Neukirchen-
Vluyn, 2014, pp 75-88.
3. Magnus Striet, 'Ius divinum – Freiheitsrechte. Nominalistische Dekonstruktionen in
konstruktivistischer Absicht', in Stephan Goertz and Magnus Striet (ed.), *Nach dem Gesetz
Gottes. Autonomie als christliches Prinzip (Katholizismus im Umbruch 2)*, Freiburg im
Breisgau, 2014, pp 91–128, esp. pp 104-105.
4. In relation to historical studies on the death penalty from a theological perspective, see
Alberto Bondolfi, 'Ecclesia non sitit sanguinem. Die Ambivalenz von Theologie und
Kirche in der Frage nach der Legitimation der Todesstrafe', in A. Bondolfi, *Helfen und
Strafen. Studien zur ethischen Bedeutung prosozialen und repressiven Handelns (Studien
der Moraltheologie 4)*, Münster 1997, 103-121; Bernhard Schöpf, Regensburg, 1958. A
condensed but informative account can be found in: Oliver Michael Timothy O'Donovan,
'Todesstrafe', in *Theologische Realenzyklopädie 33* (2002), pp 639-646.
5. See Plato, *Gorgias*, 525b-526b, quoted from: *Platonis Opera III*, edited by John Burnet,
Oxford, 1903.
6. See Clement of Alexandria, *Stromata* I 27,171,4, quoted from *Stromata* I-VI, edited
by Otto Stählin, re-edited by Ludwig Früchtel (*Griechische Christliche Schriftsteller,
Clemens Alexandrinus II*), Berlin, 4th ed, 1985.
7. See Plato, *Gorgias*, 525d.
8. See Ambrose of Milan, *Epistola* 25,3 (1040B), quoted from *Patrologia Latina* XVI,
edited by Jean-Paul Migne, Paris, 1845.
9. For a detailed account, see Daniel E. Doyle, *The Bishop as Disciplinarian in the Letters
of St. Augustine (Patristic Studies 4)*, New York, Oxford, etc. 2002.
10. See Gerd Althoff, 'Königsherrschaft und Konfliktbewältigung im 10. und 11.
Jahrhundert', *Frühmittelalterliche Studien* 23 (1989), 264-290.
11. Matthias Schmoeckel, *Auf der Suche nach der verlorenen Ordnung. 2000 Jahre Recht
in Europa – ein Überblick*, Cologne, 2005, p. 105.
12. See the great penal code of Gregory XVI, 'Regolamento sui delitti e sulle pene', in
Sergio Vinciguerra (ed.), *I regolamenti penali di Papa Gregorio XVI per lo Stato Pontificio
(1832)*, Padua 2000, pp 83-121.
13. Karl Härter, 'Vom Asylrecht zum politischen Asyl. Asylrecht und Asylpolitik im
frühneuzeitlichen Alten Reich', in Martin Dreher (ed.), *Das antike Asyl. Kultische*

Grundlagen, rechtliche Ausgestaltung und politische Funktion (Akten der Gesellschaft für griechische und hellenistische Rechtsgeschichte 15), Cologne, 2003, pp 301-336, quotation p. 311.

14. On this section, see Arnold Angenendt, *Toleranz und Gewalt. Das Christentum zwischen Bibel und Schwert*, Münster, 5th ed., 2009, pp 245-262.

15. Rainer Forst, *Toleranz im Konflikt. Geschichte, Gehalt und Gegenwart eines umstrittenen Begriffs*, Frankfurt am Main, 5th ed., 2017, p. 65.

16. Klaus M. Girardet, 'Die Konstantinische Wende und ihre Bedeutung für das Reich. Althistorische Überlegungen zu den geistigen Grundlagen der Religionspolitik Konstantin d. Gr.', in Ekkehard Mühlenberg (ed.), *Die Konstantinische Wende*, Gütersloh, 1998, pp 9-122, quotation from p. 100.

17. Friedrich Prinz, 'Der Testfall. Das Kirchenverständnis Martin von Tours und die Verfolgung der Priscillianer', in *Hagiographica* 3 (1996), 1-13, quotation from p. 9.

18. Vgl. Arnold Angenendt, *Toleranz und Gewalt. Das Christentum zwischen Bibel und Schwert*, p. 250.

19. See Jörg Trelenberg, *Das Prinzip 'Einheit' beim frühen Augustinus (Beiträge zur historischen Theologie 125)*, Tübingen, 2004, p. 137.

20. On the idea of political Augustinianism, cf Henri-Xavier Arquillière, *L'augustinisme politique. Essai sur la formation des théories politiques au Moyen-Âge*, Paris, 2nd ed., 1955. On its practical effects, cf Martin Rhonheimer, *Christentum und säkularer Staat. Geschichte – Gegenwart – Zukunft*. Mit einem Vorwort von Ernst-Wolfgang Böckenförde, Freiburg im Breisgau, 3rd ed., 2014, pp 70-74.

21. For a detailed account, see Sascha Ragg, *Ketzer und Recht. Die weltliche Ketzergesetzgebung des Hochmittelalters unter dem Einfluß des römischen und kanonischen Rechts (Monumenta Germaniae Historica, Studien und Texte 37)*, Hannover, 2006.

22. See Ambrose of Milan, *De vocatione gentium* 2,1 (1105D), in *Patrologia Latina* XVII, edited by Jean-Paul Migne, Paris, 1845.

23. See William J. Hoye, 'Die Wahrheit des Irrtums. Das Gewissen als Individualitätsprinzip in der Ethik des Thomas von Aquin', in Jan A. Aertsen and Andreas Speer (ed.), *Individuum und Individualität im Mittelalter (Misellanea Mediaevalia 24)*, Berlin, etc., 1996, 419-435, esp. 423.

24. Hans Joas, *Die Sakralität der Person. Eine neue Genealogie der Menschenrechte*, Berlin, 2011, p. 106.

25. Joas, *Die Sakralität der Person*, p. 86.

26. Joas, p. 98.

27. Angenendt, *Toleranz und Gewalt*, p. 139.

28. See Karl Gabriel, *Christian Spieß and Katja Winkler, Wie fand der Katholizismus zur Religionsfreiheit? Faktoren der Erneuerung der katholischen Kirche (Katholizismus zwischen Religionsfreiheit und Gewalt 2)*, Paderborn, 2016, p. 301.

Contributors

MARKUS BÜKER, theologian. From 2004 to 2012 in Bogotá, Colombia engaged in ecumenical peace work and accompaniment of basic Christian processes. Since 2012 at MISEREOR. Main areas of work: Concepts and critique of the development, role and influence of religion on the transformation processes. Lecturer at the RWTH Aachen University. Previously involved in development cooperation in Colombia and in international education and solidarity work in Switzerland.

Address: MISEREOR, Mozartstraße 9, 52064 Aachen, Germany.
Email: markus.bueker@misereor.de

ALINA KRAUSE has been studying the master's program Theology and Global Development at the RWTH Aachen University since October 2017, where she has already completed the Master of Education in Catholic Theology and Spanish for vocational training (2011-2017). She has been at MISEREOR, Aachen, since 2017.

Address: MISEREOR, Mozartstraße 9, 52064 Aachen, Germany
Email: alina.krause@misereor.de

DIRK MESSNER is Director of the Institute for Environment and Human Security of the United Nations University, EHS-UNU. He is also is also the Co-Chair of the German Advisory Council on Global Change (WBGU).

Address: UN Campus, Platz der Vereinten Nationen 1, D-53113 Bonn, Germany
Email: girndt@ehs.unu.edu

MARTIN EBNER, priest of the diocese of Würzburg, studied theology in Würzburg, Tübingen and the École Biblique in Jerusalem, doctorate (1991) and habilitation (1997) in Würzburg, 1998-2011 professor of exegesis of the New Testament in Münster, since 2011 in Bonn.

Research interests: historical Jesus, Christian communities in their religious and cultural environment, Gospel of Mark, Lord's Supper,

Methodological discussion.
Address: Seminar für Exegese des Neuen Testaments, Johannisstraße 8-10, D-48143 Münster
Email: martin.ebner@uni-bonn.de

MARGIT ECKHOLT, Professor of Dogmatics with Fundamental Theology at the Institute for Catholic Theology of the University of Osnabrück.
Address: Institut für Katholische Theologie, Universität Osnabrück, Schlossstrasse 4, 49074 Osnabrück, Germany
Email: margit.eckholt@uni-osnabrueck.de

FELIX WILFRED is founder-director of the Asian Centre for Cross-Cultural Studies, Chennai. Earlier he was Dean of the Faculty of Arts and Chairman of the School of Philosophy and Religious Thought, State University of Madras. Until June 2018 he was President of the International Theological Review *Concilium* and has been a member of the International Theological Commission of the Vatican. He was on deputation by the government of India as ICCR Professor of Indian Studies, Trinity College Dublin and has also been a Visiting Professor at the universities of Nijmegen, Münster, Frankfurt am Main, Boston College and Ateneo de Manila.

Recent publications include the ground-breaking *Oxford Handbook of Christianity in Asia*. Other seminal publications include *On the Banks of the Ganges* (2002), *Asian Dreams and Christian Hope* (2003) *The Sling of Utopia: Struggles for a Different Society* (2005) and *Margins: Site of Asian Theologies* (2008).
Address: Asian Centre for Cross-Cultural Studies, 40/6A panayur Kuppam Road, Sholinganallur Post, Panayur, Chennai – 6000 119, Tamilnadu, India
Email: felixwilfred@gmail.com

MICHELLE BECKA, Professor of Christian Social Ethics at the Theological Faculty of the University of Würzburg. Research interests: Fundamental questions of social ethics, ethics in prison, political ethics (migration), legal ethics, ethics and interculturality. Publications: 'Punishment and rehabilitation. Accompanying an Ethics of the Correction',

Forum Sozialethik Vol. 16, Münster 2016. 'Fraternity and Justice in the Context of Migration', in: *Thiel, Marie-Jo, Philadelphia –The Challenge of Fraternity*, Münster 2018. 'Comités de ética en elégimen penitenciario', in: Eijk, Ryan et al. (Ed.), *For Justice and Mercy. International Reflections on Prison Chaplaincy*, Tilburg / Amsterdam 2016, 121-130.

Address: Katholisch-Theologische Fakultät, Julius-Maximilians-Universität Würzburg, Raum 106, Paradeplatz 4, 97070 Würzburg, Germany
Email: michelle.becka@uni-wuerzburg.de

DANIEL FRANKLIN PILARIO is professor at the St. Vincent School of Theology, Adamson University, Quezon City, Philippines. He is the author of *Back to the Rough Grounds of Praxis: Exploring Theological Method with Pierre Bourdieu* (Leuven, 2005). As member of the Congregation of the Mission, he ministers in a garbage dump parish in Manila.

Address: St. Vincent School of Theology, 221 Tandang Sora Avenue, P.O. Box 1179, 1151 Quezon City, Philippines
Email: danielfranklinpilario@yahoo.com

LINDA HOGAN is professor of ecumenics at Trinity College Dublin. Her primary research interests lie in the fields of inter-cultural and inter-religious ethics, social and political ethics, human rights and gender.

Recent publications include K*eeping Faith with Human Rights*, Georgetown University Press, 2016 and *Feminist Catholic Theological Ethics: Conversations in the World Church*, Orbis Press, 2014, edited jointly with Agbonkhianmghe Orobator.

Address: Irish School of Ecumenics, Trinity College Dublin 2, Ireland
Email: lhogan2@tcd.ie

STEPHAN DE BEER is Director of the Centre for Contextual Ministry at the University of Pretoria, and teaches Diaconate and Community Development in the Department of Practical Theology. His own specialization is in the field of urban theology and community transformation, and he has a particular focus on spatial justice, housing and homelessness. Before he joined the University in 2013, he worked with an ecumenical community organization – the Tshwane Leadership Foundation – responding to inner city vulnerability and change in Pretoria.

Address: University Pretoria, Lynnwood Rd, Hatfield, Pretoria, 0002,

Theology Building, Hatfield Campus, University of Pretoria / South Africa
Email: stephan.debeer@up.ac.za

GEORG STOLL has studied philosophy, theology and religious studies and has been working in development policy at MISEREOR for twenty years. He is currently a member of a cross-sectional team on global urbanization.
Address: MISEREOR, Mozartstraße 9, 52064 Aachen, Germany
Email: Georg.Stoll@misereor.de

LORENA ZÁRATE studied history in her hometown of La Plata, Argentina. Since 2000, she joined Habitat International Coalition (HIC) in Mexico City and is currently HIC President at the global level. She has been involved in work on the World Charter and the Mexico City Charter for the Right to the City. She collaborates closely with the UN Special Rapporteur on the Right to Adequate Housing and is currently co-coordinating an international project to promote the Global Platform for the Right to the City.
Address: Habitat International Coalition (HIC), Huatusco 39, Col. Roma Sur - 06760, México D.F.
Email: lorenazarate@yahoo.com

MARCO KUSUMAWIJAYA is an architect and urbanist based in Jakarta. He has founded and been working with NGO's on urban sustainability, housing and justice in many parts of Indonesia and some locations in Southeast and East Asia. He had also worked in reconstruction of 23 communities in Aceh after the 2004 tsunami following persistent people-driven approach. His experiences in arts include chairing the Jakarta Arts Council (2006-2010), curating exhibitions and artists in residency programs and advisory functions in several countries. He is currently chair of the Coastal Management Committee of Jakarta Governor's Delivery Unit charged with developing policies and overseeing recovery of Jakarta coastal areas.
Address: Jl. Cikini Raya No.37b, RT.16/RW.1, Cikini, Menteng, Kota Jakarta Pusat, Daerah Khusus Ibukota Jakarta 10330, Indonesia
Email: mkusumawijaya@gmail.com

LUIZ KOHARA, member of the Gaspar Garcia Centre for Human Rights and adviser to the Centre for Support to Social Initiatives (CAIS). Popular educator, master in urban engineering, doctor in architecture and urbanism and post doctorate in the areas of urban sociology and housing.

Address: Centro Gaspar Garcia de Direitos Humanos, Rua Dom Redó, 140, Ponte Pequena, 01109-080 São Paulo – SP, Brazil
Email: luizkohara@gmail.com

MICHEAL SEEWALD born in 1987, Professor of Dogmatics and Dogmatic History at the University of Münster and Principal Investigator at the Cluster of Excellence 'Religion and Politics'.

Address: Westfälische Wilhelms-Universität Münster, Katholisch-Theologische Fakultät, Seminar für Dogmatik und Dogmengeschichte, Johannisstrasse 8-10, 48143 Münster, Germany
Email: mseewald@uni-muenster.de

Introducing the new *concilium* website

🕊 **Read the latest issue on your computer, tablet or smartphone**

🕊 **Explore our new, searchable digital archive (2007-2018)**

🕊 **Share a free sample copy with friends and colleagues**

www.conciliumjournal.co.uk

How to access the digital archive

Full access to the archive is free for all current subscribers:

1. Email **concilium@hymnsam.co.uk** to request a website account.
2. Sign in to **www.conciliumjournal.co.uk** with the account details we send you.

Libraries and colleges: new access options

Institution subscribers can set up website access to the latest issue and the archive for staff and students via IP address authentication, EZProxy and referring URL. See **www.conciliumjournal.co.uk/libraries** for details.

Hymns Ancient & Modern

The Canterbury Dictionary of
HYMNOLOGY

The result of over ten years of research by an international team of editors, The Canterbury Dictionary of Hymnology is the major online reference work on hymns, hymn-writers and traditions.

www.hymnology.co.uk

CHURCH TIMES

The Church Times, founded in 1863, has become the world's leading Anglican newspaper. It offers professional reporting of UK and international church news, in-depth features on faith, arts and culture, wide-ranging comment and all the latest clergy jobs. Available in print and online.

www.churchtimes.co.uk

Crucible

Crucible is the Christian journal of social ethics. It is produced quarterly, pulling together some of the best practitioners, thinkers, and theologians in the field. Each issue reflects theologically on a key theme of political, social, cultural, or environmental significance.

www.cruciblejournal.co.uk

JLS

Joint Liturgical Studies offers a valuable contribution to the study of liturgy. Each issue considers a particular aspect of liturgical development, such as the origins of the Roman rite, Anglican Orders, welcoming the Baptised, and Anglican Missals.

www.jointliturgicalstudies.co.uk

---

magnet

Magnet is a resource magazine published three times a year. Packed with ideas for worship, inspiring artwork and stories of faith and justice from around the world.

www.ourmagnet.co.uk

For more information on these publications visit the websites listed
above or contact **Hymns Ancient & Modern:**
Tel.: +44 (0)1603 785 910
Write to: Subscriptions, Hymns Ancient & Modern,
13a Hellesdon Park Road, Norwich NR6 5DR

Concilium Subscription Information

April	**2019/2:** *Populism & Religion*
July	**2019/3:** *Technology: Between Apocalypse and Integration*
October	**2019/4:** *Christianities and Indigenous Peoples*
December	**2019/5:** *Queer Theologies: Becoming the Queer Body of Christ*
February	**2020/1:** *Contextual Theologies Facing the Challenge of Global Violence*

New subscribers: to receive the next five issues of Concilium please copy this form, complete it in block capitals and send it with your payment to the address below. Alternatively subscribe online at www.conciliumjournal.co.uk

Please enter my annual subscription for Concilium starting with issue 2019/2.

Individuals
_____ £52 UK
_____ £75 overseas and (Euro €92, US $110)

Institutions
_____ £75 UK
_____ £95 overseas and (Euro €120, US $145)

Postage included – airmail for overseas subscribers

Payment Details:
Payment can be made by cheque or credit card.
a. I enclose a cheque for £/$/€ _____ Payable to Hymns Ancient and Modern Ltd
b. To pay by Visa/Mastercard please contact us on +44(0)1603 785911 or go to www.conciliumjournal.co.uk

Contact Details:
Name ....
Address ....
....
Telephone .... E-mail ....

Send your order to *Concilium,* **Hymns Ancient and Modern Ltd**
13a Hellesdon Park Road, Norwich NR6 5DR, UK
E-mail: concilium@hymnsam.co.uk
or order online at www.conciliumjournal.co.uk

Customer service information
All orders must be prepaid. Your subscription will begin with the next issue of Concilium. If you have any queries or require Information about other payment methods, please contact our Customer Services department.